Computers
in
Insurance

Computers in Insurance

MICHAEL D. GANTT, CPCU
ALAN J. TURNER, CPCU
JAMES GATZA, D.B.A., CPCU

Second Edition • 1985

AMERICAN INSTITUTE FOR
PROPERTY AND LIABILITY UNDERWRITERS
720 Providence Road, Malvern, Pennsylvania 19355

First Printing • July 1985

Library of Congress Catalog Number 85-71316
International Standard Book Number 0-89463-044-X

Printed in the United States of America

Preface

Why was this book written when there already are many excellent texts on computers in business? The problem, appropriately enough, was that of information overkill. Most texts on computers in business provide more detail than required by persons in the insurance industry. This book is based on the assumption that the reader is not a computer specialist but needs to know just enough about the field to make sensible use of computer resources.

This book's treatment of the subject was dominated by the learning objectives of two Institute courses—CPCU 7 – Management and MGT 43 – Managerial Decision Making. The design of each of these courses calls for three assignments on the subject of computers and information systems in a course primarily devoted to another subject. The ideal computer book for these courses would offer a self-contained subject treatment. It would trim the subject to its most essential facets and connect these to insurance practice.

Many hands helped shape the final product. Mike Gantt laid the foundation and completed the first draft. When Mike's career interests shifted, Jim Gatza took up the hammer. Four reviewers provided critical help beyond measure: Grover Brown, Director of Fire Policy Services Operations, Farmers Insurance Group; Charles Hirth, Director of Systems Training, Fireman's Fund Insurance Company; Dr. Walter H. Klein, School of Management, Boston College; and Walter A. Rhulen, CPCU, President, Electronic Tabulating Corporation. They did far more than debug the manuscript: they made positive suggestions of great value.

Four CPCU instructors participated in a field test of the next-to-last version of this text. They are Dr. Donald Burke, Dr. Conrad Kasperson, Forrest Kohler, CPCU, AIM, and Dr. Russell Waite. Their comments have contributed to the finished product and we are grateful to them and to their students for allowing the field test to add a complication to their educational efforts.

While we are indebted to these persons for their help, we bear full responsibility for this treatment of a vibrant field. We hope that this text will be out of date soon.

Michael D. Gantt, CPCU
James Gatza, D.B.A., CPCU

v

Preface to the Second Edition

Surprise! The first edition did not go out-of-date as soon as expected. This happy result reflects Mike Gantt's wisdom in distinguishing between fundamental developments and latest wrinkles.

Alan J. Turner, CPCU, accepted the task of writing this revision. He took the suggestions of others, added his considerable expertise in insurance automation, inserted a generous measure of creativity, and produced a well integrated result. To him belongs the credit for the technical and educational progress of this revision. To him go our thanks for making it up-to-date despite the dizzying rush of new developments in its subject field.

We are grateful for the valuable suggestions of the persons who critically reviewed the draft of this revision:

> J. Patrick Campbell
> Nationwide Insurance
>
> Michael C. Dowling, CPCU
> Fireman's Fund Insurance Companies
>
> John W. McCauley
> The McCauley Company

Undeniably, automation is a major force in our lives: it seems to reach every cranny. We hope that this guidebook to insurance automation provides understanding useful beyond its boundaries.

> Dr. James Gatza, CPCU
> Vice President
> American Institute for
> Property and Liability Underwriters

Table of Contents

CHAPTER 1

The Computer

EDUCATIONAL OBJECTIVES

Define or illustrate the major hardware and software terms.

Describe the basic types and functions of computers.

State the various capabilities and limitations of computers.

Describe and illustrate the following major hardware components of a computer system central processing unit, input/output devices, and supporting devices.

Differentiate between the various types of computer programming languages, including the distinction between systems software and applications software.

Describe the development of computers in terms of generations.

Describe the three major classifications of computer systems.

Define local area networks.

CHAPTER 1

The Computer

INTRODUCTION

Effective management of computers within the insurance organization (or for any organization for that matter) requires an understanding of the fundamentals of computer operations. Many people are often turned away from the study of computers by technical details that seem overwhelming. A patient analysis of the basics, however, will have a long-lasting pay-off because, like it or not, the computer is now as much a fact of everyday life as rush-hour traffic (and sometimes just as appealing).

How much information on computer equipment and operations do insurance people need? There are those who believe that managers or insurance technicians need to know a great deal. Others believe that insurance people need to know very little about computers and their operations. The first view is wrong, if for no other reason than that it is impossible for many to have a great deal of knowledge about computers. The field is developing at such a rapid pace that even people who work in the computer industry can be experts in only one or two areas.

But if it is wrong to say that insurance managers or technicians need to know a great deal about computers, it is equally wrong to say that they do not need to know much at all. Obviously, they need to know enough to allow them to use and manage computer resources wisely. They need to know, basically, the way a computer works. Perhaps the operation of an automobile offers an analogy. It is not necessary to know all about the mechanical components of a car and their operations in order to drive a car. But a basic understanding of

3

major components and how they work is a great help. With the knowledge, it is possible to make sensible operating decisions and understand malfunctions. The knowledge provides a certain peace of mind.

This chapter will try to strike a balance between providing too much information and not enough. (The bibliographical references will provide ample resources for those desiring further study.)

A CONCEPTUAL VIEW

Defining the Computer

What is a computer? The American National Standards Institute offers this definition:

> *Computer*—a data processor that can perform computation, including numerous arithmetic or logic operations, without intervention by a human operator during the run.[1]

Unfortunately, this definition raises more questions than it answers. It will be useful to think of a data processor as a type of machine and a run as the sequence of computational steps to be performed on the data. The word *program* denotes the instructions for the run or, loosely, the run itself.

A computer, therefore, can be distinguished from other information handling machines (e.g., adding machines) by its ability to hold an *internally stored program* (i.e., a sequence of computational steps). It is the internally stored program, or instructions for a run, that eliminates the need for intervention by a human operator during that run.

An adding machine is *not* a computer because each calculation requires human intervention. To rate an automobile policy using an adding machine, for example, it is necessary to take the machine through a sequence of steps. It is not possible to simply give the required rating factors and hit a key telling the adding machine to "rate" the policy. The adding machine cannot "remember" formulas. With the internally stored program, a computer can "remember" the steps to take in the rating formula.

It might be worthwhile to note that some of the new electronic calculators now on the market are computers when they can be "programmed" to perform specified operations. Granted that their capabilities are severely limited when compared with business computers, they demonstrate that "size does not a computer make." In addition, a computer is not restricted to any particular shape or function.

Adding to the confusion is the fact that numerous different terms are used for the computer field. These include, but are not limited to: *automatic data processing (ADP), electronic data processing (EDP), data processing (DP),* and *information processing.* Although textbook authors have tried to maintain specific and slightly different definitions for these terms, most people in the business world use them almost interchangeably. The term *computer science* may be one exception to this. Although this term also refers to the field of computers, its use has been restricted to the study of computers and their operation as opposed to the management of them in business organizations.

The rapid increase in capabilities and the widespread distribution of computers have contributed to the semantic tangle. Definitions can suddenly become obsolete with the development of new equipment or concepts.

Types of Computers[2]

It is possible to classify computers in many ways. In this section, we will use three approaches for classification.

Analog or Digital Analog computers are those that measure continuously variable data. The name analog comes from the fact that measurements recorded are "analogous" to the actual data in question. This is best understood by example. One of the most common examples is the speedometer in an automobile. The pointer represents the rotational motion of the drive shaft. The miles per hour figure, therefore, is analogous to the rotation of the drive shaft. Where the need exists for continuous, or constant, measurement of some process or quantity, analog computers work best.

Digital computers perform computation on noncontinuous, discrete data (i.e., they use digits). They measure only in the sense that they count in exact figures. For example, if a computer is to add up the total amount of money received in a day by the business, a digital computer would be used. The computer would add up all the individual receipts and arrive at a discrete answer (e.g., $1,080.22). It is now impossible to shop for a wristwatch without being confronted with the choice between the traditional analog kind (with hands that move continuously) and the more recent, digital-reading models.

Although analog computers are used in business (mainly in building maintenance systems), they are primarily used for scientific purposes. Obviously, most insurance organization computers are digital computers. After all, the premium invoice needs to state the specific amount due (e.g., $101.50), not display a gauge with a needle pointing just to the right of 100. It should be noted that hybrid computers, combining digital and analog features, do exist but are limited in number. This is probably going to be true of every computer classification used. There are always going to be items that bridge categories; fortunately, they will normally be the exception rather than the rule.

Special Purposes or General Purpose   A digital computer can be designed as a special purpose or general purpose machine. As you might expect, the *special purpose computer* is designed with one specific function in mind. Because of this, the special purpose computer can perform its task in an extremely efficient manner. Its disadvantage is, of course, that it can fulfill no purpose other than the one it was designed for. For example, some fast food restaurants have computerized cash registers. Each item on the menu has a corresponding button on the register. These machines speed customer service, reduce arithmetic errors, control inventories, and perform other functions. They do these things well, but are virtually useless for other applications.

The *general purpose computer* can perform different functions by running different programs. It cannot be as efficient as a special purpose computer performing a given task, in the same way that an all purpose cleaner is not likely to clean glass as well as a glass cleaner. Its virtue lies in its flexibility. It is this flexibility that makes the computer economical in many cases. Even with the availability of personal computers, it is unlikely that an insurance agency would dedicate one computer for rating and printing policies, another for collecting payments, and yet another for payroll, since each personal computer can be programmed to handle all of these tasks. Obviously, then, the general purpose computer is the dominant one in insurance industry installations.

Scientific Uses or Business Uses   Computer design requirements for scientific usage differ in nature from those for business usage. A little reflection will reveal some of the major differences. A scientific user, who may not actually be a scientist, is frequently concerned with formulas and simulations of the real world. Scientific work can involve hundreds, even thousands, of complex calculations or slight alterations to a basic formula. Computers can take the drudgery out of these and other tasks by performing the many repetitive computations for the researcher. The researcher is probably not going to be interested in documenting a large number of intermediate calculations. The researcher will be interested in the final results. Some examples of scientific uses in the insurance industry are developing rates, evaluating loss reserves, and the construction of computer models for planning.

Conversely, business uses generally require little in the way of sophisticated computation but a great deal of input and output. Policyholder billing, for example, requires a computer that determines the amount owed and prints a bill. No calculus or geometry is required—just a little arithmetic and a great deal of printing.

This text will concentrate on digital, general purpose, business-use computers.

Computer Functions

Discussion now turns to the mechanical processes performed by or within a computer. In a mechanical sense, the computer reads, stores, and writes information. It performs calculations, and it controls these operations as it performs them.

Data and information are both raw materials and products of computers. In this sense, the computer reminds people of themselves (though, it is hoped, not in any other sense). People collect information, process it, and come up with some result. The computer, however, is unable to read a book, at least in the way people read one. It is unable to view a sunset or hear a symphony. In short, the ways in which it can collect information are extremely limited. Although many different types of devices exist to collect information for the computer, they must reduce that information to a particular form, *binary form*. Within the computer, each individual circuit can be in only one of two states. That is, each circuit is either on or off, positive or negative—no other possibilities exist. This might seem like a very limited arrangement, but, in fact, it is quite effective.[3]

All data (the numbers, letters and special characters contained on a computer keyboard) are represented in this binary manner within the computer. A punched card, for example, is read by the computer in this way: a scanner "looks" for holes at a series of locations in the card. A hole is either there or it is not (the binary concept). Depending on where the hole is located in the card, a value is derived. All data are built up from this basis. A particular circuit represents a bit (short for binary digit) by being on or off. Decimal numbers and letters of the alphabet are represented by specific combinations of bits. For example, CPCU is represented as 11000011 11010111 11000011 11100100 when stored in binary form by large IBM mainframe computers. All data must exist in this form before the computer can perform any calculations or even store the data.

Once the form data must take within the computer is known, it is possible to look at the basic functions performed by the computer.[4] Keep in mind though, that only professional systems programmers work with binary representation of data, and even then, infrequently.

Read (Input)   A computer reads data in order to begin solving problems. In fact, the computer must also read in the program (program instructions are just another form, albeit a special one, of data) that prescribes the operations to be performed. Computer terminals, disk and tape drives, and other devices are used to collect or read information. Regardless of the device, the information reaches the computer in binary representation. Information read by the computer is called, of course, input.

Write (Output)   When the computer is finished processing a given input, it will write or produce the output. Various devices are used for the output function. The printer and computer terminal are the most familiar, but output does not have to be in humanly readable form. The output could be, for example, a magnetic tape, floppy disk, or possibly even a set of punched cards which will later be input for another computer operation.

Store (Storage)   A computer needs to store information until needed. Recall the definition of a computer. It is the ability to store that differentiates a computer from other information handling machines. The computer has the capability to store a sequence of computational steps (i.e., an internally stored program) as well as the ability to store data for computation.

Calculate   Once data and instructions have been read and stored by the computer and before the answer can be written, the answer must be calculated. This may be either an arithmetic $(1 + 1 = ?)$ operation or logic (is 5 greater than 4?) operation. Computers add, subtract, multiply, divide, and perform any formulas provided in the form of instructions. They also perform logical comparisons between values (for example, this operation must be repetitively performed when the computer "sorts" lists into alphabetical order).

Control   This last major function of the computer has been implicit in the discussion of all the others. The operations of reading, writing, storing, and calculating must be controlled. There must be order in the machine or else it will begin to read when it should write or store when it should calculate. Some of this control is designed into the circuits of the computer, while the rest is provided by the instructions in the programs running on the computer.

Components of the Computer System[5]

The computer itself—that is, the physical machine—exists as part of a larger system. This system can be divided into three basic categories, each with its own characteristics.

Hardware The term hardware refers to physical machines, including the computer itself. The *central processing unit* (CPU) is the heart of the computer system. It is sometimes called the mainframe. It is here that all control and calculation functions take place. Input and output devices are also considered hardware. All input and output devices are contained in the same "box" as the CPU or connected to it by cable. The CPU delegates the reading and writing of data to the input and output machines. In addition to these machines, there are supporting devices which are attached to these machines and perform various "housekeeping" functions for the primary devices already mentioned. We will study all of these in greater detail later in this chapter.

Software A stored program is the set of instructions that tell a computer which steps to take and in which order to take them. It also tells the computer which data to read, and, at the proper time, which data to write. The term *software* includes all the programs used to run the computer. These instructional programs can be divided into two categories. Programs used to perform operations necessary to the basic operation of the computer are called *system software* or the operating system. The operating system makes the hardware work. For example, MS-DOS is the operating system used in many microcomputers. Programs applying to specific problems being processed in the computer are called *application software*. Lotus 1-2-3 is the name of a popular application software program.

In an insurance company, programs dealing with insurance matters and company matters would be considered application software. System software would include programs dealing with the operation of the computer itself which would be scarcely known beyond the confines of the data processing department. Both kinds of software have increased greatly in prominence over the past few years. There are many reasons for this, not the least of which is the steadily decreasing cost of hardware per unit of storage. In this environment the question becomes, "How much software can we purchase or develop to take advantage of lower hardware costs?"

Peopleware Although the terms software and hardware are widely used, the term peopleware has yet to catch on (perhaps with good reason). This term refers to all those people who design, program, and operate the various elements in the computer installation. The typical data processing staff consists of systems analysts, programmers, console operators, managers, and others. Computers have produced a whole new profession—the persons who manage, control, and operate them. People who work in this profession are often considered to have basic characteristics different from those associated with other professions. Some of the complexity and mystique of computers has been imputed to the people who work *with* them. In many companies, these people constitute a huge and powerful department. This department controls a critical resource (information) and reports to the highest level of the organization. As a result, Data Processing or DP departments are changing their name and mission to Management Information Systems or MIS. (The next chapter will describe computer staff positions in greater detail.)

Capabilities[6]

It is important to have a conceptual understanding of what computers can and cannot do in order to make decisions which will lead to efficient use of computers, i.e., when a computer should be used and when a computer should not be used. What are the specific capabilities of computers?

Handle Large Volume of Repetitive Tasks Accurately Much of the work that goes on in today's insurance organization is repetitive paper work. A computer can perform most of these tasks much faster than a human being can and with far fewer errors (if it is programmed correctly). The computer, fortunately, does not get "bored" with all this repetition or become fatigued by it.

Process Jobs Almost Simultaneously This feature is referred to as multiprogramming. Each job (i.e., program) has a section of the computer in which it operates. The computer does not need to complete one job before starting another. While the computer is *reading* for one program, it might be *writing* for another, and *calculating* for a third.

Although the computer can calculate for only one job at a time, control switches back and forth so fast (in nanoseconds; a nanosecond is one thousandth of a millionth of a second) that it appears to us that the jobs are being processed simultaneously—hence the phrase "almost simultaneously." "Almost simultaneous" processing of jobs is possible because some computer functions are performed faster than others. For example, computers can calculate much faster than they can read or write. Multiprogramming allows many calculations to take place while the essentially slower process of reading goes on.

Multiprocessing is another way of reducing computing time. Instead of having just one computer or processor as in multiprogramming, there are one or more computers or microprocessors in a multiprocessing system. One of the processors controls the operations of all of the others which handle specialized tasks such as doing the arithmetic calculations or filing and retrieving data.

Decision Making Computers are said to make decisions in a very limited sense. The computer has the ability to follow stored instructions, make a logical comparison, and then, based on that comparison, take a specified course of action. Computers frequently check the validity of data coming in and, then, reject data that is not valid (while telling the operator that it did so). For example, if the computer is reading a policyholder file in order to print a listing of all policyholders with property in Alaska, the computer should be programmed to reject the data if it turns out that somebody fed in a payroll file rather than a policyholder file. The built-in limitation is that the computer can only make decisions it has been programmed to make.

Arithmetic and Logic Functions The computer is well known for its ability to add, subtract, multiply, and divide. Additionally, it can determine whether a number is positive, negative, or zero. It can also compare two quantities and determine whether one is larger, smaller, or if they are equal. After performing this logical comparison it can then *branch*, or *go to*, another part of the program. It can *go to* one of a series of operations based on the result of the logical comparison. (It is this ability which allows the computer to perform "decision-making" operations.)

Customer billing can illustrate how this branching logic would operate. As each policyholder's records are read, a check is made of the current account balance. The logic would look something like this:

> Compare account balance to zero.
> If equal, go to next policyholder record.
> If greater than zero, go to billing routine.
> If less than zero, go to refund routine.

Remote Processing With the advent of telecommunications (transmitting data over telephone or teletype lines), computers have gained the ability to overcome their geographical limitations. A mainframe computer can have input and output devices hundreds or thousands of miles away. For instance, a computer terminal at an airline ticket counter in Los Angeles might be connected to the airline's computer in New York. An insurer's home office computer might be connected with that of its claim representative in Spain, with the desktop terminal or personal computer of an agent in Miami, and with a medium-size computer in its Dallas Branch. Satellite communications and other technological developments promise even more rapid growth in the use of telecommunications and remote processing.

Limitations[7]

The dissimilarities between a computer and a human being are far more striking than the similarities, although it is possible to get the opposite impression from reading much of the current literature on the subject. In fact, it sometimes sounds as if it were only a matter of time (however long) before computers are given artificial intelligence capabilities, that is, before they can carry on all the thinking processes of a human. Proper analysis of computer limitations will, however, dispel this notion.

Unable to Handle Anything Other Than Certain Quantitative, Logical Considerations The computer is not going to be able to figure out how the insurance executive should react to consumer pressure groups, nor how the underwriting manager should train underwriters, nor how the claims examiner should handle a denial of coverage. This does not mean that computer programs that act as consultants to underwriters and risk managers in interpreting insureds' needs and designing a complete risk management program are impossible in the future. Often our imaginations are challenged as a computer expert describes the many things computers will be able to do for us in the future. However, our thinking might be just as challenged to bring to mind all the things computers will not be able to do in the future.

For one thing, computers are amoral. Good and bad do not compute. Nor can computers "shoot from the hip," as people must at times do in the business world. Computers cannot be inconsistent in their actions, and yet humans often crave the inconsistency of a supervisor who is a keen observer when employees are performing well and anything but observant when employees are having an off day. The list of considerations that computers cannot deal with could go on but let your imagination take you the rest of the way.

Does Only What It Is Programmed to Do Not only is the computer limited in the type of problem it can deal with; it is further limited by its inability to do anything of its own accord or learn from its own mistakes. Trained insurance professionals can piece together a full picture of a risk, even if they have incomplete information, and then focus on the facts most relevant to analyzing the risk. Computers, because they can only do what they are told, are unable to duplicate this process.

All the horror stories about million-dollar social security checks and endless past due notices sent on paid-up accounts are inaccurately called "computer foul-ups." The computer was just the tool that made the human foul-up manifest. The fantastic speed of the computer is a two-edged sword. Just as it can print insurance policies many times faster than a typist can, it can also, once it is programmed incorrectly, produce inaccurate policies many times faster than typists can. Does this mean that the programmer's error is more "wrong" than the typist's? Of course not. But the consequences of the programmer's error are far greater.

Economic Limitations Computers are further limited in the sense that, economically speaking, they should only be used to perform functions that would be more expensive to perform by other means. If a monthly expense account takes an executive ten minutes to total, while the computer would take only 18.753 nanoseconds, it does not follow that the executive should use the computer to add the expense account. The actual computation time of a program is a small part of the total time involved—including the time to write the program, to test the program, to set up the program to run, and the time to input data. Computers should be used on those tasks that will meet the organization's business objectives and enhance the productivity of its employees.

COMPUTER HARDWARE

The Central Processing Unit (CPU)[8]

Hub of All Activity The CPU, sometimes called the mainframe or the processor, is the hub of all activity in the computer system. All calculations are performed by the CPU, and no machine in the system operates except under the control of the CPU. Input devices are used to read data. Output devices are used to write data. It is the central processing unit, however, which actually processes (performs calculations and controls) data.

Three Units The CPU itself consists of three units—the primary storage unit, the arithmetic/logic unit, and the control unit. Each unit is responsible for different functions.

Primary Storage Unit. The *primary storage unit* of the CPU, as its name implies, stores data. Specifically, it stores data that is of immediate importance to the job being run. Primary storage differs from other storage (e.g., magnetic disk, discussed under input/output devices) in that it resides in the CPU and contains only data pertinent to the program currently being run.

An analogy may be helpful. An underwriter analyzes insurance applications to distinguish acceptable from unacceptable submission. The underwriter, however, does not keep all of the insurance policies written by the company on the desk. Instead, the underwriter selects only those applications or policies with which it will be necessary to work on that day (or perhaps that morning, or even that hour). Underwriters work this way because desk space is limited and because underwriters do not need every file at one time. For similar reasons, the primary storage of the CPU is used only for data currently needed. Other terms for this storage include *main memory* or *core*. Main memory must be distinguished from *auxiliary memory* or *auxiliary storage*, terms referring to *media* that will be discussed below. The term core comes from the fact that historically computer storage in many computers consisted of a magnetic core. Integrated circuits have all but replaced magnetic cores for main memory.

Arithmetic/Logic Unit (ALU). Before a calculation is made, data is transferred from primary storage to the *arithmetic/logic unit* (ALU). After a calculation is completed, the answer is transferred to primary storage. If this sounds like some sort of "musical data" game in which the CPU spends a great deal of time moving data back and forth from one section to another, remember that the computer is very limited in its functions (it can add, subtract, multiply, divide, and compare numbers). Everything must take place according to an ordered sequence. The speed at which the computer operates more than makes up for the seemingly cumbersome and rigid internal sequence it must follow.

Control Unit. If the CPU is the heart of the computer system, then the *control unit* is the heart of the central processing unit. It controls the activities of the CPU and, therefore, of the computer system as a whole. The control unit receives and interprets program instructions from primary storage. Based on the instructions, the control unit will issue commands to the appropriate part of the computer system.

Types of Storage Media As noted earlier, data is represented in the computer in a binary state (e.g., on or off, positive, or negative). The particular physical device used in the computer to represent this binary state varies by computer and is determined primarily by cost factors. A number of devices have been used over the years. For example, some of the earliest electronic computers developed in the late 1940s and early 1950s used vacuum tubes as the medium of storage. By today's standards, these were too large and too expensive to make large computers cost-effective. With the development of cheaper storage media to replace tubes, more and more organizations have been able to cost-justify computers.

Magnetic Core. At one time, most computer systems used *magnetic core* as the medium for primary storage. A single magnetic core is a tiny doughnut-shaped ring of ferrite, capable of being magnetized in one of two states, on or off, at any one moment. The CPU contains millions of these tiny rings, strung together by wiring. The magnetic core was a major improvement over vacuum tubes, but far more dramatic developments were still to come.

Semiconductor Memory. Many of the computers produced today utilize *semiconductor memory.* Semiconductor circuits are etched in silicon chips. In one of these chips (about an eighth of an inch in area), over 256,000 binary digits can be stored. Semiconductor memory has all but replaced magnetic core for main storage because of its low cost, size, increased speed and storage capacity.

Others. Bubble memory and laser memory both offer much promise for the future. Bubble memory is based on molecular physics and laser memory is based on optics. Both of these memories will bring greater reliability, greater storage capacity in the same space, and lower cost per bit of information during the next several years.

Storage Structure The primary storage unit of the CPU is divided into four areas: *program storage, input storage, output storage,* and *working storage.*

Program storage is where the computer stores the instructions of the program it is currently executing. The program must be represented within the computer in the same manner (binary code) as data. Input storage is the place where data is stored immediately after it is read into the system by an input device. Output storage is where data is stored immediately before it is to be written by an output device. Working storage is where data that is partially processed is stored. The relative size of these four areas can be altered and controlled by the programmer.

Addressing Structure Addressing informs the computer where each of the four major storage areas starts and stops. Regardless of the medium used for storage in the computer, each unit of storage medium—that is, each individual magnetic core or each semiconductor circuit—represents a *bit.* Bits are combined to form a *byte,* which is the smallest unit in a computer capable of representing a letter, number, or any other special character present on a computer terminal keyboard. Bytes are combined to form a *word.* Some manufacturers use other terms but these are standard in the insurance industry. Each word, byte, and even bit, can be located by its address, its location with the computer. Locating a bit, byte, or word is similar to sorting mail for post office boxes. All the boxes look the same. The way to tell them apart is by counting the rows and columns or by the identifying number of each. Of course, this does not mean that every bit in the computer has a number painted on it. But the computer "counts" bits starting from the first one until it gets to the bit it needs. If this sounds time consuming and inefficient, remember that today's computers operate internally in time measured in nanoseconds (one thousandth of a millionth of a second; in other words, a billionth of a second). This tremendous speed overcomes an otherwise inefficient process.

The central processing unit, then, is the center of activity in' the computer system. From its control unit, all functions of the system are directed. In its arithmetic/logic unit, all calculations and logic comparisons are performed. Its primary storage unit holds all data currently being utilized, in magnetic core, semiconductor, or another medium. Data is located within primary storage in major storage subdivisions. Individual pieces of information, that is, bits of data, are located within the CPU by the addressing procedure.

Input/Output Devices[9]

Input devices allow computers to read information; output devices allow computers to write information. These devices are usually physically separate from the central processing unit, although they are connected by a cable through which digital signals pass back and forth. Today, *computer* generally refers to the CPU, input/output devices, and supporting devices in total. To think of the CPU as a computer would be equivalent to thinking of the human heart as a person.

An input/output device may be designed for input, for output, or for both. As each type of device is identified, the following symbols will be used: (I) stands for input only, (O) stands for output only, and (I/O) stands for input or output.

The following list of devices is by no means exhaustive. It does, however, include those devices most likely to be encountered in the insurance industry.

Operator's Console (I/O) The operator's console unit is used for giving the computer very specific instructions relevant to its basic operation. The size and functions of the console unit are determined primarily by the size of the computer.

When the computer is turned on, a few switches on the front of the CPU must be flipped, pushed, or otherwise manipulated. This will get the power flowing to the machine. The computer will then ask the operator certain questions through the console. The console may be a typewriter keyboard or a keyboard with visual display. Keyboard consoles type the questions for the operator to answer. The operator answers by typing the response. The console is used for technical input/output concerning the machine's operation, not for inputting programs or data.

Card Readers (I) and Punches (O) Many people are familiar with the punched card as a medium for carrying data. Punched cards were used in counting machines at the turn of the century. Although punched cards continue to be used, their use is decreasing.

The card is read by the input device which scans the card looking for holes. The presence or absence of holes, and the pattern made by the holes, provide binary information to the computer. Compared to other media, cards are bulky, slow to process, and have a short life expectancy. Their use is becoming restricted to specific functions for which these disadvantages are not a great liability.

The card punch (O) does just what its name suggests—punches holes in cards as it outputs computer data. Most computers using cards will have a card reader-punch which is nothing more than the two machines combined into one. Card reader-punches are classified (I/O).

Magnetic Ink and Optical Character Readers Checks usually have numbers in magnetic ink printed at the bottom, allowing them to be read by a computer. Numbers printed in magnetic ink can be detected and interpreted by an input device. Once the character has been read, it is converted into an electrical impulse (in binary form) to be used in the computer. Optical character readers (OCRs) perform in a a similar way. Some carriers print information on the return stub of the billing notice so that it can be processed by optical character readers to eliminate the manual data entry of the payment information.

Printing Devices (O) Printing output is the most common form of computer output. Computer printers differ in the means employed to produce the image on paper. Some use fonts similar to that on an electric typewriter which print a single character at a time while others use laser and electrophotographic technology to print an entire page at a time. Various printing devices are in use today and many more are being developed. Further development is sorely needed. Since printing is still basically mechanical rather than purely electronic (as are the internal operations of the CPU), it is the slowest part of the computer system. Many computer systems are held back in their processing because of the amount of printed output required. The insurance industry is particularly affected by this limitation of computer systems because of the industry's heavy printed output requirements.

Computer Output Microfilm (O) A computer output microfilmer is a device that combines electronic, photo optical, and electromechanical techniques for the purpose of converting digitized computer output into human-readable images and automatically recording these images on microfilm or microfiche. The acronym COM is often applied to such film. Some users flinch at the thought of replacing paper with film. There are factors offsetting these anxieties. A film cassette occupies less than 1 percent of the space required for a paper stock of equivalent reports, and a fiche occupies less than 0.05 percent as much space as equivalent paper. Similar proportions hold for weight. Since COM media have indexes to the material contained on them, data can be retrieved in one-ninth the time required to access a paper document.

Special I/O Devices Some devices do not fit easily into the established categories. An example is the automatic airline ticket vendor now found in some airports. The vendor is designed to accept credit cards, request flight information, and issue a ticket on the spot. Another example is the automatic teller machines now found at banks. These machines collect deposits, dispense cash, and perform other banking functions. As these special purpose units demonstrate, input/output devices can take on various characteristics and can be designed to fill almost any special need.

Terminals (I/O) *Terminals* are devices that allow the users of a computer system to gain access to (i.e., input programs and data to, and obtain output from) that system in a manner that standard input/output devices (e.g., card readers, printers) will not allow. What this most often means is that while standard I/O devices must be in close proximity to the CPU (usually within feet of each other), terminals can be almost anywhere. There must be some communication link between the CPU and the terminal—usually a telephone line. These telephone line hook-ups can be either *dial-up* or *dedicated,* sometimes called *leased* (i.e., a permanent line is installed between the computer and the terminal eliminating the need for dialing). The two basic types of terminals are *batch terminals* and *interactive terminals.*

Batch Terminals. *Batch* terminals are used in much the same way that standard I/O devices are used at the computer site. They are particularly useful when many people wish to use the computer and yet are located at a distance from it. Service bureaus, companies that process data for their clients, use this approach to provide accounting services to insurance agents. The service bureau places a terminal in the agency which is connected to the service bureau by telephone lines. Accounting information is then entered into the terminal and stored in the terminal's memory or on a floppy disk until it is sent to the service bureau all at once or in a batch.

Interactive Terminals. *Interactive* terminals differ from batch terminals in that the user does not submit an entire task or series of tasks when using an interactive terminal. Instead, the user enters requests, including program instructions or data, one line at a time. The user receives a response before entering the next statement or request, hence the term interactive. (Sometimes the term *conversational* is used to describe the same characteristic.) Terminals are often classified as intelligent or dumb terminals. An intelligent terminal provides the user with data processing capabilities, in addition to serving as an input/output device. Dumb terminals are limited to input/output.

Another way of distinguishing terminals from other input/output devices is that terminals are usually described as *remote* I/O while other I/O devices are local. Although terminals are being used more and more as high-volume data entry or input devices, they can also be used to view low volumes of output. Standard I/O devices are designed for high volumes. Since equipment terminology is used rather loosely, it is necessary to be specific when describing hardware items.

Interactive terminals are often referred to as common *cathode-ray tubes* (CRTs) or *video display terminals* (VDTs). VDTs look like television sets, but display numbers and letters produced by the computer or from the attached keyboard on their screens. The visual display of data offered by these terminals has led to their widespread acceptance. VDTs come in many shapes and sizes and are produced by many manufacturers. They enable people with no technical computer background to access information stored in the computer.

Terminals are one of the primary means of getting computer capabilities directly in the hands of underwriters, claims adjusters, agents, clerical employees, and others.

Supporting Devices[10]

Since the central processing unit is the "center" of the computer, all other devices are sometimes called *peripherals*. In addition to input/output devices, peripherals include devices used to support either the CPU or the I/O devices. Most of these machines are referred to as auxiliary memory because they provide for storage accessible to the CPU but not actually resident in the CPU.

Auxiliary Memory

Magnetic Tape. Magnetic tapes (often called "mag tapes") are long, narrow ribbons which are usually mounted on reels. There is usually 2,400 feet of tape on a reel about ten inches in diameter. As the name indicates, portions of the tape are magnetized so that data may be stored and read. The process works in a way similar to the way tape recorders work. *Tape drives* read and write magnetic tape. The major advantages of magnetic tape are its relatively low cost and its large storage capacity (over 152 million characters, or 19 million cards, on one 2,400 foot roll). The primary disadvantage of magnetic tape is the need to store and seek data sequentially. For example, if the information desired is located on the end of the reel, it is necessary to pass the entire reel of tape before the desired section can be read, obviously a very time consuming procedure. Nevertheless, magnetic tape is one of the most common forms of auxiliary memory (storage) used today.

Cassette Tape. Cassette tape is used on many smaller computers because of its convenience and its similarity to standard magnetic tape. This medium is growing in popularity and, in fact, is used for some functions on a few of the larger computers. Its sequential nature makes it ideal as a disk drive backup storage and recovery medium for mini and microcomputers.

Disks. Although disk storage is more expensive per bit of data than magnetic tape, it is better suited for finding the specific information sought from a given file quickly. Disks are called *direct access* or *random access devices*, while tapes are called *sequential access* devices.

Practically speaking, *disk drives*, the machines that contain and operate the disks, are found on most computers operating today. Disks resemble phonograph record albums (though disks have no grooves like those on phonograph records). They contain a coating of iron oxide and are written on and read in a way similar to that for magnetic tapes. The data is read by a mechanism which hovers slightly above the disk platter and detects magnetic signals.

The popularity of storage has increased rapidly in recent years as the popularity of VDTs and personal computers has created the need for large amounts of data to be immediately available, that is, *online.* Magnetic tape would, of course, be unsuitable for this purpose since it is not designed for direct access. Disk drives vary in their size, portability, and capacity for data. "Diskette" and "floppy disc" are names for inexpensive variants of the disk.

Others. Other auxiliary memory devices include *drum storage* in which data requiring extremely fast retrieval are stored on the surface of a spinning cylinder; *mass storage systems* which combine the ability to retrieve data online, although slower than disks, with the storage of vast amounts of data on spools of magnetic tape; *add-on memory* (another primary storage unit attached to the CPU to, in effect, enlarge the size of primary storage directly); and others.

What distinguishes an input/output device like a VDT from an auxiliary storage device like a magnetic tape drive? True, the CPU reads data from the magnetic tape as a source of input and outputs the results of the processing to another tape. Why, then, is magnetic tape not considered an input/output device while the VDT is? The difference between them rests mainly with their differing primary uses. VDTs are primarily used as a method for getting data into the computer. The information processed through a VDT cannot be referenced later unless the information is placed on an auxiliary storage device such as a disk or magnetic tape. In contrast, the dominant reason for using magnetic tape is to store very large volumes of data.

Other Supporting Devices   Computer rooms frequently contain more equipment than has been described here. The other machines in a computer system control the devices discussed. These are necessary because of the way the computer operates (a very "simple-minded" machine working very, very fast). These would include *channels* and *control units* (each device usually has to have a control unit to "manage" it). It is not important to know the names of these machines, only that they exist and are there to support the equipment which has been discussed. Exhibit 1-1 depicts the major hardware components in a typical computer system.

COMPUTER SOFTWARE

Software is the term for the programs that run the computer. Historically, the capacity of the hardware increased dramatically while the capacity of the software remained relatively limited. If more programs were needed, more programmers were hired. There were no radical improvements in the efficiency of programming. This is slowly changing. Still, software is often the bottleneck in the systems development process. Because of this, more attention is being given to software and, specifically, to the methods employed in its development. Software is now produced and offered for sale by an enormous number of organizations. An insurance company has the opportunity to purchase a payroll system or a complete personal or commercial policy processing system, rather than employ its own staff to produce and maintain these programs. Agents are faced with a bewildering array of competing software programs which can automate one or more functions in the agency. Almost every shopping center in the country has a store selling general purpose software—that is, software not tailored to insurance purposes. This standard software, particularly spread sheet and word processing software, has found many applications on the personal computers of insurance people.

Exhibit 1-1
Computer System

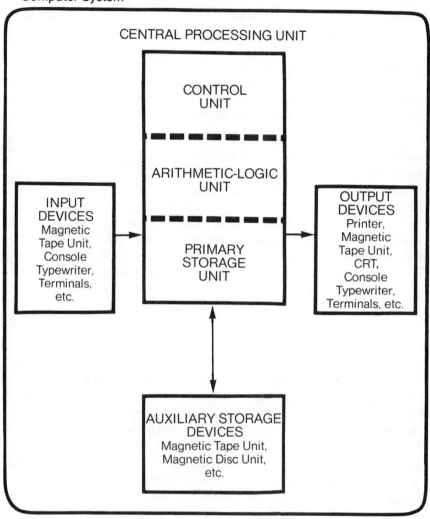

Types of Computer Languages[11]

Machine Languages The first generation of computer languages was machine language, which came into use in the 1940s and 1950s. Machine language means the language that the computer understands. Further, it is the *only* language that the computer understands. Any other language must go through a sort of "translation" into machine language before the computer can understand it.

Since the computer can only deal with information in binary form, machine language, necessarily, must be binary. It is, and, in fact, looks just like a string of binary numbers. A specific program instruction in machine language might look something like this:

110011101100110111001010000111101

This looks like a random string of binary digits. To the central processing unit of a computer, however, it could have a very specific meaning. It is the bit pattern that indicates to the computer what to do.

The first part of the instruction tells the computer what the function to be performed is (e.g., ADD, SUBTRACT, and so on) and is called the *op code*, or *operation code*. The layout of the rest of the instruction is determined by the op code, but usually includes the data to be used in performing the function or the address of the data (remember the discussion on addressing structure used in storage?) to be used in performing the function. The first computer programmers had to be quite precise in writing instructions for the computer. The work was tedious and errors were almost impossible to detect until the computer executed the instructions. Understandably, the personal computer revolution would not have occurred, if this was the only way a non-DP professional could communicate with a computer.

Symbolic Language The disadvantages associated with machine language led to the development of symbolic language, the second generation of computer languages, in the early 1950s. Someone realized that if "01001" meant "subtract" to the computer, a symbol, such as "S," might be substituted for "01001" and the computer could internally convert the "S" to "01001." Soon, each of the computer's instructions had some mnemonic code (e.g., ZA for Zero and Add, CLA for Clear Accumulator and Add). This was so much of an improvement that symbolic addresses were developed. Symbolic addresses allow the programmer to give a certain address in storage, such as ANSWER, for where the answer to a problem was stored. At the beginning of the program the programmer would specify that ANSWER referred to a certain address. After that, whenever the programmer wanted to refer to that address, he simply used the word ANSWER rather than the numerical value of the address. This saved a great deal of time and, of course, was much easier to remember. Other improvements that were later added to this type of language freed the programmer from having to give the exact address for each instruction. The programmer would now only have to specify the address of the first instruction. All other instructions would be stored according to sequence by the processor. This became a tremendous help whenever it was necessary to modify a program. In machine language, the insertion of a new instruction

The insurance agent needs to know the whereabouts of the source program! This statement needs some explanation. Many large insurance agencies have their own in-house computer systems. Rarely do these systems use software created within the insurance agencies. Instead, the software packages are purchased from and maintained by vendors. For their own protection, the vendors cannot release source programs. Like the secret formula for a soft drink the source program, carefully guarded, is the essence of what the vendor has to sell the agent. But what would happen if the vendor got out of the insurance agency software business? This might happen because the vendor lost its expertise, went out of business, or simply lost interest in the insurance agency market. If the vendor quit, the agent would be left with the agency records in a computer system whose design could not be upgraded or modified. Obviously, then, the agent does not want to purchase a software system unless the system vendor offers some protection in terms of ultimate access to the source program. The solution is an ingenious one: The source program is placed in escrow and becomes available to the user if the vendor fails to perform as specified in the contract. An insurance company (or any other software buyer) should have the same protective feature provided by the software purchase agreement.

required the renumbering of the addresses of all the subsequent instructions in the program. With symbolic language, that renumbering could be handled much more easily. With all these mnemonics, computer programs began to resemble the English language to a very limited degree. There still is a one-to-one relationship between the number of instructions in the symbolic language program and the machine language program. That is, every instruction that the programmer writes in symbolic language must be converted into a specific machine language instruction.

The software aid that translates the symbolic language program into the machine language program is called the *assembly program* or, sometimes, the *assembler*. The program as written by the programmer is called the *source program*. After it is translated by the assembly program it is referred to as the *object program*. A computer cannot process a source program, only an object program.

Procedure-Oriented Languages *Procedural languages*, the third generation, came into use in the 1960s. As their name suggests, these languages are oriented to a particular procedure, or type of problem, rather than to the logic of the machine in the way that a symbolic language is. This leads to another difference between procedure-oriented and symbolic languages. Procedure-oriented languages are generally "portable" (can be used on more than one computer); symbolic languages are not. This difference became very important when companies replaced early computers with newer, larger computers *(upgrading)* and found that new programs were going to have to be written to replace the old one. Procedure-oriented languages are designed to be run on many different computers. These programs must be translated into machine language by a software aid called a *compiler.* As mentioned earlier, the program as written by the programmer is referred to as a source program. After it is compiled, an object program is produced. The compiler and assembler can be thought of as two slightly different translators that convert programs to machine readable form. Exhibit 1-2 depicts the language translation process.

Although symbolic language is still used today for many purposes, procedure-oriented (sometimes called *high-level)* languages dominate. Symbolic language is used when efficient use of the machine is the highest priority because it is machine- rather than problem-oriented. Many personal computer and video arcade games are programmed in symbolic language because of the fast response times they are required to have. Each machine has it own symbolic and machine language, thus giving the programmer flexibility in taking advantage of the design of the machine. Procedure-oriented languages are used when the time of the programmer has the highest priority.

Common Procedure-Oriented Languages.[12] While certainly not covering all the procedural languages currently in use within the insurance industry, the following section will touch on most of them. All of them are procedure-oriented languages. They are not listed in any particular order so as to avoid giving the impression that any one language is consistently preferable to another. Each has its own advantages, disadvantages, and reasons for being.

COBOL. The most commonly used language in the business world today is COBOL (COmmon Business Oriented Language). COBOL was first published in 1960. The development of this language was actually a project carried out by a committee. The express purpose of this group, the Conference of Data Systems Languages (CODA-SYL), was to produce a language that would both serve the business community and help users achieve program compatibility (portability from one computer to another). Most computer manufacturers provide COBOL compilers for their machines. As with human languages, there

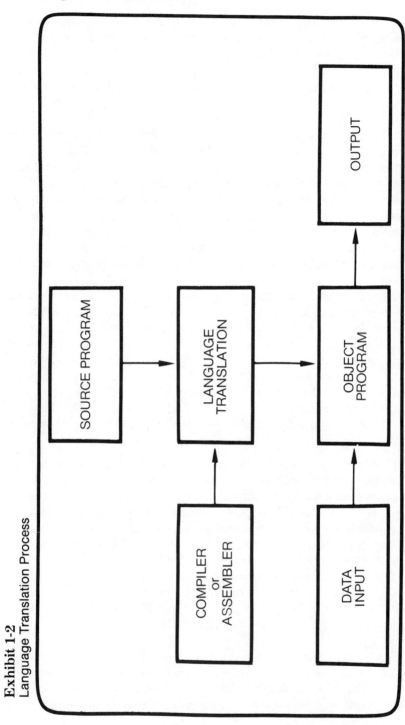

Exhibit 1-2
Language Translation Process

are "dialects" of COBOL. One of the most noticeable features of a COBOL program is that it looks something like English. There are, of course, COBOL versions in French, Spanish, and other languages.

One of the prime advantages of COBOL is flexibility. Unfortunately, this flexibility is also one of its prime disadvantages—the language itself requires no conformity in structure. Flexibility in a language is no liability to the person who writes the program. However, the person who must later revise or modify that program will have a very difficult time. Leaders in the industry have addressed this problem with *structured programming* techniques. These techniques impose a logic which programmers are encouraged to follow.

FORTRAN. (FORmula TRANslation) was developed in 1954 as a scientific-mathematic language. FORTRAN enables engineers and scientists to program the computer in familiar symbols, very similar to the language of mathematics. It caught on quickly and remains a standard language even though its use in the business world has been limited.

BASIC. Developed for college students in mid-1960s, BASIC (Beginner's All-purpose Symbolic Instruction Code) soon became popular because of its simplicity. BASIC has found its greatest use on personal computers and time sharing systems because it allows someone with little or no background to sit down at a terminal and begin writing simple problem-solving programs.

RPG. (Report Program Generator) has found its prime niche in smaller business computer operations. As its name indicates, RPG's primary purpose is to produce reports. It is not meant to be a sophisticated, highly flexible language. Rather than writing a program in a relatively free form, RPG requires the programmer to use prescribed specification sheets. Input is described on one sheet, output on another, and so on. Some programmers exclude RPG as an actual programming language, insisting that the RPG compiler produces a program from specifications given it by a programmer. Nonetheless, it enjoys common usage and more than a little respect among those who have used it.

Nonprocedural Languages[13] A nonprocedural language tells the computer *what* is to be accomplished rather than exactly *how* to do it. A compiler or interpreter determines *how* the computer should do what is asked for. For example, an agency's personal lines customer service representative might sit down at a terminal connected to the agency's computer and type

LIST ALL OF MY HOMEOWNERS POLICIES WITH LIMITS LESS THAN 300,000.

This is a complete "program." It leaves the decisions how the list should be formatted, when to skip pages, how to number pages, how to sort the insured's name and/or policy number, and what limits to use to the software. If the software makes the wrong decisions or assumptions, the statement can be made as specific as necessary to obtain the desired results.

An analogy of giving instructions to a taxi driver will help to clarify the distinction between procedural and nonprocedural languages. With a procedural language you have to tell the driver exactly *how* to proceed: "Drive 500 yards. Turn left. Drive 380 yards. Turn right. Drive to the traffic lights. If the light's green. . . ." With a nonprocedural language tell the taxi driver *what* you want: "Take me to the movie theater on Malvern Street."

Fourth-generation Languages[14] Fourth-generation languages were created for two main reasons, first so that nonprogrammers could obtain the information they need from computers, and second to speed up the programming process. Some fourth-generated languages are nonprocedural. Some are procedural but results can be obtained with far fewer instructions or lines of programming codes than with COBOL. Many contain both procedural and nonprocedural statements or instructions. Unfortunately there are no standards for fourth-generation languages yet because new computer language ideas are constantly emerging.

Now that there is the term "fourth-generation language," more than likely every new language will be called "fourth-generation" by its marketing representatives. A fourth-generation language should allow a nonprofessional programmer to obtain results with it after learning a portion of the language in not more than a two-day training class, make intelligent assumptions about what the user wants, and be designed for on-line interactive operation.

Fourth-generation languages cannot satisfy the needs for all computer applications. They are not general purpose but are more limited in application. However, these languages enable users to obtain the results they need fast, whereas traditional programming in COBOL does not.

The Application Development Process[15]

This section will describe the basic life cycle, so to speak, of the process involved in designing and building data processing applications. The process applies to insurance carriers, agency automation vendors, and even users of PC software products. As you will see, separation of development into phases is an integral part of a successful development process and an ideal method for keeping the user's desires and needs synchronized with the progress and costs of development. During the application development process, the completion of each phase adds to the knowledge about the system and reduces the risk in progressing with the next phase by:

- detailing and documenting technical and managerial expectations through which progress and change can be measured,
- allowing more accurate estimation for subsequent phases, and
- providing milestones at which approval must be obtained before continuing to commit resources to the project.

The development of data processing applications in phases is illustrated in Exhibit 1-3. Exhibit 1-3 shows the scope, schedule, and resources of a development project and the approximate effort involved in each.

Requirements Definition   The major objective of the requirements definition phase is to establish and obtain formal agreement with users on the business functions to be included and excluded in the new system, and any constraints under which the system must be designed.

Overall information requirements include a processing flow through user departments and the volumes and frequencies of inputs and outputs. Information flows or interfaces between user departments and other functional areas in the organization must also be defined.

The information produced in this phase is documented in a System Requirements Report that describes "what" is going to be done, *not* "how" it will be done. A common failing in application development is to leap too quickly into the how—before what's to be done is known and approved.

External Design   Can you imagine having a house built without seeing a "picture" of it? You could be very disappointed. One major objective of the external design phase is to define the overall system from the users' point of view, to provide a "picture" of what they will get, so to speak. Another objective of this phase is to validate that the system, as it is now defined, still meets the business requirements.

The functional information flow document describes, in user terms:

- processing flow of data from users to computer, then back to users,
- interfaces with other data processing applications, and
- functions performed on the data sent.

The functional information flow provides the users with a "picture" of the system being developed. With it, they should have enough information to determine if the system will meet their needs.

Exhibit 1-3
Phased Development Approach

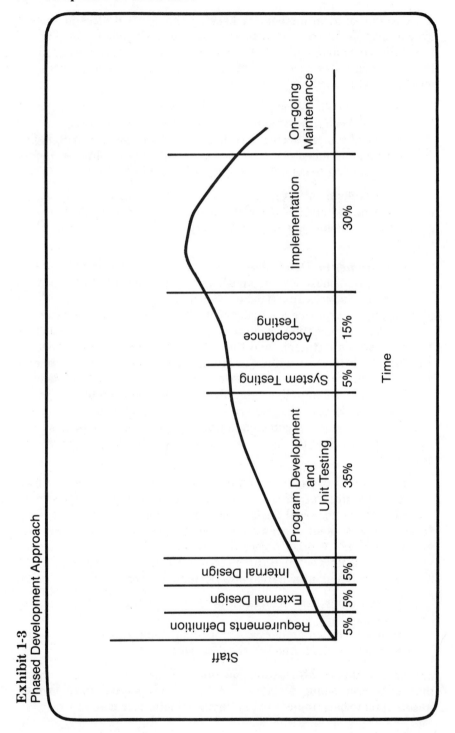

Once this effort is completed and approved, DP is on solid ground with respect to a technical plan and approach. They are less likely to encounter extension rework. DP has a documented, approved baseline from which change can be controlled. In short, this phase is used to plan for what will be happening next.

Internal Design   If the major objective of external design was to present a user view of the system, it follows that internal design must construct a data processing viewpoint of the system. The major objective of this phase is to develop enough detail to provide a precise blueprint—just as in building a house—to plan and estimate implementation.

This is evident from the documents produced during this phase. Program functional specifications describe what is to be done at a level necessary to plan and estimate the programming required. Data file specifications include definition of the data bases, data files, records, and data elements to be used by the system.

Usually, the external and internal design phases are performed as one funded project. The information produced in these phases is documented into major sections of a System Design Report.

So what does all this do for DP and the users? Defining and approving user requirements is the first step to specifying external design. Only when the external design is known and approved can you determine the computer configuration and data processing approach needed to support it.

Program Development   The objective of the program development phase is to build and test each component of the system and to ensure that the components fit together into an integrated system. During this phase program specifications detailing how functions are to be performed are prepared. Only at this point is the programming language selected. Programs are written and then individually tested to ensure that the program works as specified. Rough drafts of the user and operator manuals are developed for use during the system and acceptance test phase.

This phase usually requires the most development effort. Because of this, it is important to be specific in defining the objectives and expected results of this phase before it starts. This helps avoid the low productivity and extensive rework that often results from incomplete planning and definition.

System and Acceptance Testing   The objective of the system test phase is to test what was developed in the previous phases: to subject the system to a variety of stresses and conditions, and to verify that the system and documentation meet the design specifications. Acceptance testing is carried out by the end users to ensure that the system works within the business environment and satisfies their needs. These tests do take time, but it is time well spent.

At the end of this phase the user and operator manuals have been tested and the installation and training plans documented. The system is now *operable;* it performs according to the expected results documented for the system test cases.

Installation The objective of the installation phase is to convert and process live data in the new system. A large installation may be phased in over a period of time. In fact, the larger the system the more elaborate the installation plan. The system is now operational; it is in working order; it performs according to expectations using live data. The maintenance documentation developed during this phase will facilitate any future modifications.

Types of Software

We have discussed the various types of computer programming languages and where they are utilized in the application development process. The software "pie" can be sliced in a different way—into system software and applications software. In general, systems software is that which is primarily concerned with the operation of the computer. Applications software is primarily concerned with solving problems.

Systems Software Systems software includes the operating system—the group of programs that operate the computer. The operating system controls the use of other programs. Program libraries are stored on an auxiliary memory device, usually a disk, and are called upon when needed. For example, the library may contain a program that produces a report of written premiums classified by the insurance agency that produced the business. The original program was probably written by a programmer sitting at a CRT. Once debugged and tested, the program is stored in the computer's program library. Whenever the program is to be run, the operator calls upon it by name—that is, the operator needs to type only a few characters into the operator's console to retrieve the program and start running it.

Compilers which translate procedure-oriented language into machine language are a type of systems software. Another common type of systems software used with interactive terminals is the teleprocessing monitor. This type of software operates under the control of the operating system and acts as a mini-operating system for those programs being utilized by the interactive terminals. The very nature of processing with interactive terminals requires some additional systems software to remove detail from application programs.

Applications Software A program to produce automatically rated homeowners policies is an example of applications software. A program to produce a report of all premiums and losses within a given territory is another illustration of applications software. So, too, are the word processing, file management, and spreadsheet programs available for personal computers. Systems software can be thought of as overhead while applications software provides a more immediate payoff. Neither is more important than the other, for they exist in mutual dependence. Applications software exists to solve problems and produce output while systems software exists to support that process.

In general, applications software uses procedure-oriented languages. This makes the programming process more accessible to the user.

THE DEVELOPMENT OF COMPUTER TECHNOLOGY[16]

The development of computer technology is usually expressed in terms of generations. Unlike human generations, where it is fairly easy to distinguish one generation from another (father and son are always two different people), computer generations have somewhat arbitrary lines of demarcation. Progress now seems to be steady. Still, a technical breakthrough might cause a giant leap to a new era, and people will then say that a new generation of computers is here. One reason for these varying views is that computer manufacturers gain an obvious marketing advantage through announcing the birth of a new generation of hardware.

The First Generation (1951-1958)

Although the first electronic computers were developed in the mid- or late-1940s, the first generation is said to have begun with the development and installation of the first business computer. This machine was a UNIVAC (UNIVersal Automatic Computer) developed by the Remington Rand Corporation. IBM entered the field in 1953 with its model 701. These first generation machines used vacuum tubes as their primary elements. The equipment was noted for its bulkiness and noise. Only machine language was available at this time.

There were few programmers and they needed a very intricate knowledge of the particular machine's operation. Programming early machines was a very time-consuming practice and therefore, computers were first used in applications offering high cost saving. Initial applications were commonly in payroll, billing, or inventory.

Few companies could afford the early computers. A mystique surrounded the machine at the time. Many people feared that the computer would eliminate their jobs. Most of the companies who purchased early computers did so for other than purely economic reasons. Some wanted the prestige associated with having a computer. Others desired to become familiar with computers to be able to take advantage of improvement as they occurred.

The first generation was a time for computer manufacturers and users to "get their feet wet." False starts occurred and developments often changed directions. It was during this early era that IBM took the lead in the computer field from Remington Rand.

The Second Generation (1958-1964)

Though the transistor was invented in 1948, it took ten years for the transistor to be perfected and used on production computers. The second generation of computers was born with the introduction of IBM's 1401 and 7070 computer. Transistors replaced vacuum tubes in these and similar computers. Magnetic core was used for main memory. Magnetic tape and disk were common as auxiliary storage devices.

During this era, computers became less of a novelty and more of a serious business tool. They were used to perform a growing variety of clerical functions. The development of symbolic languages, or assemblers, made the process of programming less tedious. Procedure-oriented languages such as COBOL came into common use. The fear of the computer began to disappear as people realized that computers could create jobs as well as eliminate them.

Most of the applications computerized during this time were said to be *batch processed*. Data were grouped into batches and then processed by the computer. For instance, processing each policy on the computer separately would have been very inefficient for insurers using this generation of machine. Instead, policies were combined into batches and the computer would process an entire group of policies as one run. Second generation machines were therefore often referred to as batch processors and their era as that of batch processing. Batch processing is still common. However, during the second generation it was the prime mode of processing while today it is only one of several.

The Third Generation (1964-1971)

With the announcement of the IBM 360 series of computers, the third generation of computers was born. The 360 was offered in different models, each possessing varying degrees of processing power. These and other computers like tham were distinguished first of all by their use of integrated circuits which, because of their smaller size, allowed for faster processing and greater storage capacity in the same physical area. There were more changes associated with the introduction of the third generation than simply technological improvement. The IBM 360 itself was designed to replace all of IBM's previous computers (with a few exceptions). In fact, its name, 360, came from a reference to the 360 degrees of a circle. This machine was to go "full circle" in filling business and scientific needs. Other major developments also occurred.

Standardization There was tremendous pressure for the computer manufacturers to standardize their products. Once you bought a computer, you were probably "locked in" to the equipment made by the manufacturer of that computer. Equipment made by other firms could rarely be used with the computer purchased. Programs were not yet transportable from computer to computer. Buying a new computer often meant that existing programs were made obsolete. Customers, led by the largest computer customer of the time, the federal government, exerted sufficient pressure on the manufacturers to induce much standardization in the third generation.

Timesharing Timesharing involves the use of a computer terminal in an interactive mode. Timesharing has now come to generally mean sale of computer time to a user who obtains access to that computer with a terminal. The user pays only for the processing time utilized. This makes large computer capabilities accessible to small organizations.

Multiprogramming Multiprogramming is the term used to describe the computer's ability to process several jobs, or programs, "almost" simultaneously. This function was not available until the advent of the third generation. Multiprogramming allowed the computer to become much more efficient internally and thereby speed up processing.

Expanded Input/Output The third generation saw the development of many more input and output devices. Not only were more media introduced, but they were offered in a greater variety of models. Users could now purchase equipment more exactly fitted to their particular needs.

Particularly noteworthy was the development of computer terminals in significant quantity and quality. This enabled computer users to proceed from the batch-only processing of the second generation to the batch or interactive processing of the third generation. The term online is used interchangeably with interactive in this context. It reflects the fact that interactive processing requires one's input/output device (terminal) to be physically connected to the computer (usually by cable).

Procedure-Oriented Language Third generation machines were designed for greater use of high-level languages. Languages like COBOL and FORTRAN gained widespread use with these systems. Although each manufacturer had a slightly different version of COBOL, conversion standards emerged. Programming took on greater importance during this time. The major focus of software development was to make the most efficient and productive use of the computer as possible.

Minicomputers Minicomputers will be discussed at greater length later in this chapter. At this point, it is interesting to note that the first commercial minicomputer was developed at about the same time as the large system IBM 360. Minicomputers, much like remote terminals, served to get a manageable "chunk" of computer power closer to the person who needed it.

Prior to the third generation, computers did one thing at a time very, very fast. With the third generation they were able to do many things concurrently (i.e., almost simultaneously) very, very, very fast.

The Fourth Generation (1971-?)

Although there is a fair amount of agreement about when the first and second generations ended, opinions differ with respect to the end of the third generation. IBM's 370 computers offered significant improvements over their 360 predecessors, but disagreement exists as to whether those improvements constitute a fourth generation. A description of the improvement might bring this question into clear focus.

Advanced Circuitry New developments occurred in this area at a torrid pace. Improvement in silicon chip technology allowed greater and greater storage capacity in the same physical area. Semiconductor memory offered far greater capacity than magnetic core storage. It seemed that almost every announcement of a new computer proclaimed more memory at lower cost.

Increased Multiprogramming Multiprogramming, introduced in the third generation, matured in the forth. Remote terminals proliferated throughout organizations. Larger systems with more and more diverse users required more sophisticated use of the multiprogramming methodology.

Virtual Memory Although this concept was developed earlier, it was not until the fourth generation that it came into common use. Virtual memory is a technique that allows auxiliary storage to be treated as primary storage. Effectively, this offers more capacity in primary storage for the programmer without actually increasing primary storage in a physical sense. That is why it is called "virtual" memory. The auxiliary storage device used for this concept is normally a disk drive since it has capacity for direct access.

Microprogramming This refers to the technique of controlling various functions of the computer with pseudo-instructions already integrated into the computer circuits. This function is provided by the manufacturer and adds flexibility and speed to the computer system.

Increased Information Storage This has been perhaps the one most significant characteristic of fourth generation machines. With the growing use of computer terminals, the value of online storage capacity became even greater. This meant more auxiliary storage, primarily in the form of disk, a medium uniquely suited to this requirement.

Rather than being merely processors, replacing clerical workers, fourth generation computers become information handlers, providing information and performing new functions. The rapid decline in the cost of computer power made many new applications cost-effective. Fourth generation computers extended computer power throughout the organization.

The Fifth Generation (?)

The second, third, and fourth generations of computers were each an extension of the previous generation, implemented with dramatically better technology. Fifth generation computing, as defined by the Japanese when they began their own efforts under that title in 1981, is to employ so-called *artificial intelligence* techniques and new computer designs to make computers easier to use and able to mimic several characteristics of human intelligence. The hope is to make machines that can speak and understand verbal communications, make inferences, and generally deal with "knowledge" instead of raw numbers and letters.

Expert systems are the leading commercial application of artificial intelligence today. Expert systems already in use imitate the performance of human experts in areas such as medical diagnosis and oil exploration. IBM is experimenting with an expert system to take over the burden of responding to some of the messages a computer's operating system sends to the computer operator, sometimes as many as 300 a minute. The system currently runs on a mainframe of its own. Clearly the fifth generation is just dawning, if the Japanese definition is used.

Some believe that we are already into the fifth generation. The distinguishing characteristic of the fifth generation is *executive aid*, according to this group. That is, the computer will be used more and more extensively by managers in the day-to-day decisions of the business. It will be common for the manager to have a computer terminal or workstation at his or her desk. Using a user-oriented language, he or she will ask questions about activities throughout the organization. The manager will also be able to ask "what if" questions of the computer—for example, what would happen to premium income if two rating classifications were combined?

Sure to expand widely in the fifth generation is the role of *data communications* (often referred to as *telecommunications* or *teleprocessing*) whereby data is transferred from one terminal or processor to another terminal or processor. Satellite communication techniques are now in use and are expected to grow even more. Data communications costs are expected to decline. The benefits are not without dangers. For instance, *electronic funds transfer* (EFT), allowing money to be transferred by use of a credit card, eliminates the need for checks and offers much convenience. But the potential for harm is significant.

The one factor constant in every aspect of computers of the fifth generation will be "more": more capacity, more speed, more options, and more complexity. Exhibit 1-4 presents one summary of the stages in computer evolution.

COMPUTER SYSTEMS

The term computer and computer system have grown synonymous, and we will use them that way here. Somehow, computer system seems more appropriate, if for no other reason than the connotation of complexity. To understand anything of great complexity we tend to divide it up into pieces of more manageable size. "Divide and conquer" might be a suitable battle cry for those who wish to understand the field of comuputers. Computer systems will be divided three ways—by size, by response time, and by structure.

Classifying by Size[17]

At one time, the sole measurement of a company's progress in computer usage was the size of the computer itself. This is no longer true. Computers are becoming not only bigger and faster; they are also becoming smaller and faster. Sophisticated computer users now normally have a proliferation of computer equipment, including multi-

Exhibit 1-4
Facets of Computer Evolution

Name	Period	New Hardware	New Software	New Functions	Organizational Location	Effect on Organization
Gee whiz	1953-1958	Vacuum tubes, magnetic records	None	Initial experimental batch applications	Controller's department	First appearance of technicians (with salary, responsibility, and behavior problems); automation fears among employees
Paper pushers	1958-1966	Transistors, magnetic cores	Compilers, input/output control systems	Full range of applications, inquiry systems	Proliferation in operating departments	EDP group proliferation; some workers and supervisors alienated or displaced; introduction of new rigidity but also new opportunities
Communicators	1966-1974	Large-scale integrated circuits, interactive terminals	Multifunction operating systems, communications controllers	Network data collection, remote batch processing	Consolidation into centrally controlled regional or corporate centers with remote terminals	Centralization of EDP organization; division data visible to central management; some division managers alienated; response times shortened
Information custodians	1974-c. 1982	Very large file stores, satellite computers	General-purpose data manipulators, virtual machines	Integration of files, operational dispatching, full transaction processing	Versatile satellites instead of terminals, with control still centralized	Redistribution of management functions, with logistic decisions moving to headquarters and tactical decisions moving out; resulting reorganization; field personnel pleased
Action aids	c. 1982-?	Magnetic bubble and/or laser-holographic technology, distributed systems	Interactive languages, convenient simulators	Private information and simulation systems, inter-company linkages	Systems capabilities projected to all parts of organization; networks of different organizations interconnected	Semiautomatic operating decisions; plans initiated by many individuals, leading toward flickering authority and management by consensus; greater involvement of people at all levels; central EDP group shrinkage

ple computers of various sizes, from pocket calculators to mammoth systems occupying a floor or more of huge buildings.

The important development is that every computer customer or potential customer now has a broad range of computers, differing in design and operation as much as in size, to choose from. As this trend continues, classification of computers by size should become more difficult, while the chances of a company finding the computer of "just the right size" should increase.

Microcomputers   Microcomputers can be best defined as single-user, low-cost computers that sit on top of a desk or workstatioh. Since microcomputers are also referred to as personal computers (PCs), the two terms will be used interchangeably throughout the book.

The development of the silicon chip in 1971 made the first microcomputer possible. The chip was originally designed to be the "brain" in small, handheld electronic calculators, but it has since been adapted to many other uses. The heart of the microcomputer is the microprocessor—a miniature central processing unit complete with arithmetic/logic unit, input/output control logic, and registers for storing data. The technology of microcomputer design offers staggering possibilities. New techniques are expected to reduce chip logic densities by a factor of 100 or more which would mean that 1 or 2 of these silicon chips could emulate today's large CPU.

During the last several years, personal computers have become a common sight in insurance companies and agencies. Insurance industry employees from company executives to clerical workers are using microcomputers for preparation of reports and budgets, chart and graphics generation, project management, word processing, personal and commerical lines rating, financial modeling, statistical analysis and other previously time-consuming manual tasks. Personal computers are also providing basic agency automation support of client and policy information as well as the agency's marketing programs.

Microcomputer proliferation within the insurance industry is a result of the many benefits they offer. Personal computers are increasing employee productivity and enriching the jobs of both clerical and professional employees. By simplifying budgeting and other analytical tasks, micros are permitting the assignment of these tasks to secretaries and administrative assistants, allowing managers to use their own time more effectively. Personal computers are also more cost-effective than the intelligent terminals connected to the mini and mainframe computers they often replace. The word processing, mass storage, and data processing capabilities of micros simply do not exist in the intelligent terminal. Micros are also being used for local data entry and error checking. When used for these tasks, data can be collected and stored for data transmission to company mainframe computers from agency and company offices at predetermined intervals or on demand. Local processing reduces the processing load on company mainframe computers, lengthening the intervals between mainframe upgrades. Microcomputer based local processing also avoids the down time and slow response problems periodically experienced by users of mini and mainframe computers. Finally, PCs allow managers to perform complex analyses, answer "what if" questions, and provide a range of decision support functions.

Minicomputers Minicomputers are multi-user computers requiring their own floor space for CPU, computer memory, disk drives and printers. Digital Equipment Corporation produced the first commercial minicomputer in 1965. Originally considered a fad, or, at most, an extremely small segment of the market, minicomputers have gone on to become a mainstay of the industry. Minicomputers offer the following advantages and disadvantages.

Flexibility. As general purpose computers, "minis" can perform many different functions, such as rating, sales analysis, or word processing.

Adaptability. Minicomputers, like the large-scale or mainframe machines, are also adaptable. The many peripheral devices available to minicomputer purchases today offer the ability to "mix and match." The cost of a typical minicomputer system could range from $2,000 to $100,000 or more, depending on the number of devices (input/output, auxiliary storage, and so on) used.

Relative Low Cost. Compared with large-scale or mainframe computers—especially those which existed when minicomputers were introduced—the cost of "minis" made computers accessible to many more people. This new product actually enlarged the computer industry by making computers available to smaller users, especially insurance agents, who previously were prohibited from taking advantage of automation because of the cost involved.

Ease of Use. The third generation started the use of sophisticated operating systems. Although this software offered many benefits to large computer users, it also tended to add a great deal of overhead. This overhead often led to inefficiency in the operation of the computer. Large data processing departments evolved where only a few programmers had been needed before. This put more and more people between the computer and those who originally wanted the computer. The minicomputer cut through all this by taking a small version of the computer and putting it with the people who needed it.

Communications. Minicomputers can function not only as computers, but also as terminals. The Data communications technology developed to allow minicomputers and large-scale computers to "communicate" with each other in a network. This feature enabled the minicomputer to cope with one of its disadvantages—its limited storage capacity. To access large data files, the minicomputer could be "hooked up" to a large-scale computer (in this context, referred to as the host computer).

Physical Nature. Large-scale computers were notorious for their tremendous weight and for their space requirements. Paradoxically, they had to be handled with kid gloves because of their sensitivity to temperature and humidity conditions. Minicomputers were both smaller and more rugged. They could be put close to where the work was performed. Ironically, this happened at the time when many organizations built elaborate showcases in which to house their computers. Moreover, minicomputers, because they were smaller, did not produce the tremendous heat of the larger machines (which is of more than minor importance for people who must work in the same room with one).

There are also disadvantages to minicomputers, however.

Simplistic. There are many jobs which are too complex to be handled by minicomputers.

Limited Storage. Storage size is, of course, much less for a minicomputer than for a large-scale computer.

Slower Execution. Instructions are generally executed at a slower speed in minicomputers. This is not as much of a disadvantage as may first appear, however, since there is not as much going on internally (operating system software) as in the larger machines. Besides, a user's main concern should be the overall throughput of the machine (how much total work is accomplished in a given time) and not the number of nanoseconds it takes for one instruction to be executed.

Less Powerful Capabilities Overall. The net result of these disadvantages is that a minicomputer is less powerful than a large-scale or mainframe computer. Minicomputers are being designed with more storage capacity and faster execution speeds—some are becoming comparable to large-scale systems in these respects. But, practically speaking, these cease to be minicomputers, as that term is generally understood. With the rapid development of microcomputers and the proliferation of computers of all sizes, the term may well become an anachronism by the 1990s. If so, it will certainly be remembered as one of the most popular "buzzwords" of the 1970s.

Large-Scale or Mainframe Computers   Mainframe computers are so large that they require a separate room for the computer itself and the memory, disk and tape drives, printers, and environmental systems necessary to support them. These include the IBM 370 line and the Burroughs 7000 series of computers. The extremely popular IBM 360 series also fits into this category, although technological advances and attendant price reductions per unit of computer power make the 360 appear feeble compared to newer equipment in this class.

The IBM 370 line of computers is probably the single most popular computer series in the insurance industry today. It comes in various sizes and models, allowing it to fill the needs of both very large and fairly small insurance firms. Since the introduction of the original IBM 370 line, IBM has announced two new series of main line business computers designated as the 303X and 308X series. More major announcements by IBM and other manufacturers are expected to occur almost routinely in the years ahead.

The characteristics of large-scale computers include the following.

Heavy Support.   Investments in computers of this size provide computer manufacturers with the incentive and funds to offer a wide range of supporting services. These include, but are definitely not limited to, full-time specialists to assist in the most technical aspects of computer operation, software consulting, long-range planning assistance, seminars, advance education, and meetings with other users.

High Speed Printers.   Printers that produce 2,000 lines of print per minute are not uncommon with large-scale computer systems. Printers using laser and electrophotographic technology can print up to 120 lines per page and 167 to 526 pages or over 20,000 lines per minute.

Large Disk Storage.   These systems are noted for their large capacity for data. The disk is the most common medium for the masses of data that are now being stored.

Communications Ability.   Today's large-scale computers are being designed with ease of telecommunications as a key feature. Operating systems have grown in size and complexity to such an extent that they can control a large sophisticated network of computers and terminals.

Multiprocessing.   While multiprogramming was the running of two programs concurrently, multiprocessing is running two or more processors simultaneously. The IBM 3084, for example, links four powerful computers in parallel processing. These central processing units can operate in tandem, in which case they are called "twin CPUs." The duplication of critical computer hardware results in a system which is capable of continuing operation while failing portions are isolated and repaired. It is also possible to have multiple processing units which are different in size and capacity.

Off-Loaded CPU. Off-loading the CPU means removing functions normally performed by the central processing unit and putting them in some supporting device. A front-end controller is used to control certain aspects of the network.

For example, the CPU must maintain "constant" communication with each terminal so that when someone requests information from the terminal, the CPU can respond. To maintain "constant communication, the CPU checks with the first terminal to see if there is a message to be sent. If not, it goes to the second terminal in the network (each terminal is assigned an address). After the CPU has checked each terminal, it starts over and checks them all again. This continuous process is called polling. The computer's speed makes it seem as if there is "constant" communication with the terminals. The need for off-loading arises because each time the CPU checks a terminal, it is executing instructions and using up valuable time. If a front-end controller is used for polling, when a terminal does request information from the CPU, the front-end controller (sometimes called front-end processor) simply "passes" the request on to the CPU. The front-end processor can be a single purpose machine or a minicomputer can be used to perform this function.

Classifying by Response Time

The concepts of batch processing and online processing have already been described. This section will elaborate on each and explain how these two different modes of processing coexist in many computer installations.

Batch Processing In the batch processing mode, data is converted into some computer readable form, gathered into batches, and then taken physically or telecommunicated periodically to the computer for processing. This "period" could be every hour, every day, or every week; most often, it is every day or overnight. Turnaround time is quite slow when compared with online processing, but for many purposes batch processing works quite well. Most important is that it makes efficient use of the computer's time: computers work most efficiently on large volumes of similar data that can be processed sequentially.

Batch processing was the most common form of processing in the second generation and during the early part of the third generation. As time went on, computer speeds and capacities increased, and data processing costs decreased relative to employee costs, managers questioned whether the efficiency of the computer was more important than the efficiency of the people using it. For example, overnight processing dictated that any error made by someone in the punched card would not be detected until the computer could *edit* it. It is common practice for data entry personnel to check one another's work by rekeying the same information. This is called *verifying*. This process catches some of the errors before the data enters the computer for processing. Because errors detected by computer edit were not returned to the person making them until the following morning, worker efficiency was sacrificed. A data entry operator could make one mistake and, because the computer would not catch it until that night, might go on making the same mistake on subsequent work processed that day. It is psychologically better to detect errors and correct them as soon as possible.

During the early 1960s, many companies were computerizing new functions such as inventory control, billing, and order follow-up. The computer produced monthly reports and the like in a clearly satisfactory manner, but did not provide fast access to data that was completely current. The parts warehouse with computerized inventory could have a listing of all items in stock, but it would only be as current as the last batch run. The accounts receivable report of an insurance broker was similarly out of date on most working days. The computer system was not as good as the old manual system in this respect. With batch processing, the ability to go "directly to the file" was limited.

Online Processing It would be inaccurate to say that online processing chooses human efficiency over computer efficiency. Instead, online processing offers a more desirable balance between the two. The term online signifies a direct, current link with the computer. This usually implies the presence of a VDT. However, it can be another device as commonplace as the telephone. Ordinary touch-tone telephones can be used by customers of many banks and saving institutions as terminals, with the buttons providing the means for telling the computer what bills to pay. Obviously, telephones are slow and limited in flexibility when compared VDTs.

To say that one is online with the computer does not specify the functions the terminal is able to perform. The system design can provide a highly limited capability, such as policyholder data verification. On the other hand, remote terminals can be given full capability to retrieve, add, and change any data in a policyholder file.

Online processing was a boon to many computer users, including programmers. They can maintain their programs by using a terminal located near their desks. Other users, too, are eager to take advantage of the potential provided by online terminals. A terminal allows remote use of at least a portion of the organization's computer. It also allows rental of a terminal and purchase of service from a vendor's computer (timesharing).

Real-time processing is a specific type of online processing through which the user not only has direct access to the computer and its files, but can also modify or use those files immediately and directly. Real-time processing exists when information is processed in time to be used in a business transaction. A familiar example is the airline reservation computer. Space availability is checked, space committed, and the ticket issued while the customer waits at the ticket counter. As you might expect, only a portion of online processing is real-time processing.

When online processing became a practical reality for many companies in the third and fourth computer generations, did they abandon batch processing? No, because adopting the online mode did not require abandoning batch processing. Many applications are still processed most efficiently in the batch mode.

Hybrid Processing Hybrid processing combines features of batch and online processing. A data entry operator may use a VDT terminal for data input, an element of online procesing. The computer holds the data on some auxiliary storage device (that is, tape or disk) until a sufficient number have accumulated, and then proceses the data, thus providing an element of batch processing. Hybird processing is the basis of many insurance company personal and commercial policy processing systems.

Classifying by Structure

Centralized Data Processing[18] Centralized data processing, as contrasted with distributed data processing, concentrates the processing of information in one or a few locations. A centralized automation policy seeks to distribute data processing in a manner that maintains managerial control over information. Data processing activity and growth are kept under control by a central data processing department which uses one or more mainframe computers to service a network of terminals. Centralized data processing, because of the economies of scale it provides, can justify the purchase of expensive hardware and software. With the centralization of data processing, management can monitor adherence to its standards for system design, quality, compatibility and auditability, as well as keeping track of the organization's overall automation policy. Centralized data processing is oriented toward top-down control, control of computing costs, control of computing uses, and, in some cases, control over the information being processed.

Excessive centralization of data processing can result in the creation of bureaucracy that fails to meet user requirements for information. Centralized DP operations also tend to grow lazy and may fail to exploit new developments. A prime example is the personal computer's backing by non-DP departments in many firms.

Extreme centralization has technical dangers. As the network of terminals connected to the central host computers grow in size and complexity, terminal response time decreases. Another drawback is the total unavailability of terminal usage when the mainframe fails.

Distributed Data Processing (DDP)[19] DDP distributes computer "intelligence" throughout the computer network rather than having it all at the host computer. The development of the minicomputer was one of the prime forces facilitating DDP. Minicomputers, and now microcomputers, are located in the branch or department of the user to perform some processing functions and to communicate with the mainframe. Decentralized data processing is oriented toward bottom-up productivity improvement; improved exploitation of automation for departmental tasks and the design of systems to meet user needs.

There are a number of pitfalls involved with DDP. Applications which process a large mass of data and data with high security requirements must be processed centrally. If not carefully controlled, DDP can result in the incompatibility of data because the same data has a different definition in each location or because the disks used in one computer cannot be used in another. Creeping escalation of machine costs is another drawback to DDP. The first DDP application is often easy to install. As new applications are added, complexity, main memory requirements, the number of terminals, and auxiliary storage requirements increase.

Best of Both Worlds The centralization versus decentralization debate is not one over an either/or issue. Properly addressed, the issue can provide the best of both worlds. The proliferation of micros as stand-alone personal workstations, a pitfall of uncontrolled decentralization, has raised the question of how to share data among incompatible micros, minicomputers, and mainframe computers. Insurance industry employees do not work in isolation. Even though they use a personal computer, they still want to be able to retain some of the benefits provided by a centralized system including the ability to exchange messages with their co-workers and to access information from several computer files while preparing a document or analyzing data. How can centralized and decentralized micro-, mini-, and mainframe computers be made to work together?

Local Area Networks (LANs) LANs are receiving a great deal of attention as the solution to this problem. The LAN can be thought of as a high-speed data pipeline or electric highway connecting two or more computers, enabling them to share both programs and peripheral hardware.

One advantage of a LAN is that everyone on the network has access to the most recent data. The simpler, cheaper alternative to the LAN for data exchange is to make several copies of the file on floppy disks and give each user a copy. There are drawbacks to this simple solution. Many data files are too large to fit on one or two floppy disks. When floppy disks are used, their user must be careful to recycle or discard out-of-date diskettes to prevent the inadvertent use of stale information. Computer hardware costs have dropped significantly, but the cost of essential equipment such as bulk disc storage and high speed line printers remains high. Through the LAN, the high storage capacity of a hard or Winchester type disk is available to all stations on the network. This provides everyone with much faster access to the same data than would be possible with floppy disks. In addition to sharing hard disk storage, the LAN allows sharing expensive computer peripherals such as color plotters, letter-quality printers and connections between the local area network and mainframe computers.

Despite its promise as the backbone of the automated office, the LAN has been slow to develop. LAN implementation requires substantial research and planning for a company to realize full benefit. The personal workstations connected to LANs may be widely dispersed across many departments within a company. With the rapid spread of microcomputers, some companies cannot name what equipment is already in place, let alone decide how to tie them together. In the absence of accepted industry standards for the transmission media (telephone lines or coaxial cable) and for the needed high level communication software, many firms are holding back rather than committing to LANs which might not survive the test of time.

Although there is not a LAN which can currently meet the needs of most potential users, dominant LAN designs for specific applications will emerge in the next few years. As insurance company data processing planners begin to address local networking in earnest and improvements in hardware and software continue, LANs should gain widespread acceptance in the last half of the decade.

SUMMARY

This chapter began by differentiating computers from other office machines. Then, the discussion was limited to digital, general purpose computers used in business.

The chapter analyzed the basic computer functions—input, output, storage, calculation, and control. It pointed out that an overall computer system comprises hardware (the computer equipment), software (the computer programs), and people. Capabilities and limitations were cataloged.

The next section of the chapter provided a more detailed discussion of computer hardware. The central processing unit, input/output devices, and supporting devices were all covered.

Computer software was examined in terms of the types of computer languages, the languages commonly used, the process of producing a program, and software classification.

A scheme of computer generations was presented. It should be stressed that these generations are useful as a means to an end. That is, they can help make clear what has occurred to date in computer technology development and thereby offer a perspective from which to view current and coming events.

The last section of this chapter looked at today's computer systems from three different points of view: size, response time, and structure. Local area networks were then offered as one solution to the problem of getting these diverse systems to work together.

The computer is one of the primary tools of American business today. The future is likely to make this less a statement of fact than an understatement. This is particularly true for the American insurance industry. A widespread understanding of computer fundamentals will not guarantee a more effective utilization of computers, but it can be the means for achieving that end.

Chapter Notes

1. American National Standards Institute, *American National Standard Vocabulary for Information Processing*, X3.12-170, 1970.
2. Donald H. Sanders, *Computers in Business—An Introduction*, 3rd ed. (New York: McGraw-Hill, 1975), pp. 143–148.
3. James A. Senn, *Information System in Management* (Belmont, CA: Wadsworth Publishing Co., 1978), pp. 166–167.
4. Sanders, pp. 156–159.
5. Elias M. Awad, *Introduction to Computers in Business* (Englewood Cliffs, NJ: Prentice-Hall, Inc., 1977), pp. 115–119.
6. Awad, pp. 112–133.
7. Sanders, pp. 151–153.
8. Awad, pp. 117–118, 160–171.
9. Anthony Ralston and C. L. Meek, eds., *Encyclopedia of Computer Science* (New York: Petrocelli/Charter, 1976), pp. 667–707, 1404–1410.
10. Ralston and Meek, pp. 899–916.
11. Sanders, pp. 334–345.
12. Sanders, pp. 334–345.
13. James Martin, *An Information Systems Manifesto* (Englewood Cliffs, NJ: Prentice-Hall, Inc., 1984), p. 30.
14. Martin, pp. 31–33.
15. IBM, *Managing the Application Development Process—Part 1*, 1st ed. (Poughkeepsie, NY: International Business Machine Corporation, 1977), pp. 2-9–2-16.
16. Awad, pp. 72–76.
17. Awad, pp. 90–101.
18. John Leslie King, "Centralized versus Decentralized Computing," Computing Surveys, Vol. 15, No. 4, December 1983, pp. 319–348.
19. King, pp. 319–348.

CHAPTER 2

Managing the Computer

EDUCATIONAL OBJECTIVES

Describe the general organization of the departments that accomplish data processing in insurance companies and in insurance agencies.

Describe the functions of programming and systems analysis.

Describe the major challenges faced by computer managers.

Describe the major kinds of vendors of data processing services and the services they provide.

Explain the role of end users in the management of information in an organization.

Describe the components of the cost and value of information.

Differentiate among various information management concepts.

Explain the progress and problems involved in the development of an organization's Management Information System.

Explain the concept of *database* and describe the objectives of database management.

CHAPTER 2

Managing the Computer

INTRODUCTION

Chapter 1 concentrated on the computer itself and the systems development process. This chapter will focus on the people and activities around the machine. This difference is comparable to that between reading a technical manual on the operation of an Army tank and reading a description of how the tank can be used in battle. The former is worthwhile as a means to understanding the latter.

Chapter 1 discussed the rapid development of computer technology and the fact that changes are happening at an increasing rate. Chapter 2 will examine the effects of this rapid development on the people who manage the computers and the information they facilitate. This rapid pace places tremendous demands on managers and employees and goes a long way to explain many shortcomings in effectively managing the computer. It certainly helps to explain why even good solutions in computer management often have a short life span. As a result, the future of computer management is viewed with less than total confidence in the ability to predict and handle what the future may bring.

In recent years there has been a shift of focus from computer management to information management since the early days of computerized data processing. Persons associated with the computer were originally charged with managing that computer. As more and more work was taken on by the computer, this approach gradually changed. Those involved in computer work began to see their jobs not as managing the computer, but as managing the information of the company. This seemed a logical conclusion since computers were only

53

the means to an end, and they saw that end as information. American business has given almost unanimous approval to this approach. The approach is often reflected in the title of the department that houses the computer. Early names were "Data Processing," "Automatic Data Processing," and "Electronic Data Processing." Today such names as "Information Services," "Information Processing," and "Management Information Services" are much more prevalent. Information management has become a distinct management field.

Management Information Systems (MIS) have been the subject of much discussion. Generally, this concept represents the desire to see one all-encompassing management information system in an organization. In this context, computer systems are part of a larger whole. Some believe that the MIS approach is the best approach; others see it as an elusive ideal unattainable by mortal man. There are many who do not accept either of these opinions. This wide range of opinions makes management information systems an interesting topic.

THE COMPUTER DEPARTMENT AND ITS PEOPLE

All of us have become "computer people" to some extent. That is, everyone has had to adapt to the computer in business. (Personal life has not been immune to this change, but those considerations are beyond the scope of this discussion.) People now request "input" rather than the opinions of others. People now use a "systems approach"— rather than common sense—to solve problems.

People who use computers are called *users*. The term's meaning varies, however, depending on who is using it. For example, for workers in the data processing department, all the other departments in the company are user departments, and all the other employees are users. From the point of view of the computer operator, however, everyone else is a user—including programmers. Adding to the confusion, computer vendors (that is, computer manufacturers) consider all their customers, including the operators, as users. To understand the specific meaning of the term, therefore, it is necessary to show it in context. This text will use the relatively common term *end user* to apply to all users other than the data processing department. In other words, the term end user is reserved for those people for whom a specific computer use is intended.

There has been a large growth in the number of people working in the field of computers. There has been an impressive division of labor, too. The first uses of computers in business were usually rather simple batch-processing tasks. For example, one of the most common uses of early business computers was to replace old accounting machines that had been used to produce monthly billings. There was little need for a large staff of computer programmers, systems analysts, operators, managers, and others then. But as computer power grew, more and more people were required. And as computer sophistication grew, more and more division of labor was needed. One of the first areas where this occurred was in programming. With the earliest computers, programmers actually operated the machines. After writing a program, programmers would process it on the computer, and then review the results. Soon it was realized that programmers could be more productive if all they did was write programs. Someone slightly less skilled could be hired to operate the computer. As the next section will show, the computer operator's job has also gone through several divisions.

A better understanding of the people who manage the computers is important if we are to derive the full benefits of computer equipment. The very first step toward such an understanding is to shed all stereotypes or preconceived views of computer people. Computer programmers are as varied in personality as are insurance underwriters, agents, or company presidents.

Insurance Carrier Computer Operations

When used in a data processing context, the term operations refers to the department charged with the responsibility of physical maintenance, operation, and security of the computer itself. In many companies this department has been given the title *data center*. Other similar titles are common. The staff will be referred to in this text by a number of names: data processing, information processing, or computer staff.

Development Operations began as part of the data processing department. The position of *operator* was considered less desirable than some of the other jobs in data processing. This was appropriate in the days prior to advanced operating systems, data communications, multiprogramming, and other features requiring significant operator activity. Picture an operator at that early time. An operator might be asked to run, for instance, the monthly customer billings. Under the previous manual system, that process might take ninety-five person-hours. The computer might take four hours for the same job. From a business perspective, this meant a dramatic increase in productivity. But from the point of view of an operator, it meant that once the data had been loaded into the computer (through cards or some other means), it was four hours before the computer could do anything else. College students often held these positions because they could study during the long operating runs and therefore accepted a relatively low salary.

Change came with the advent of multiprogramming, under the control of sophisticated operating systems. In addition to the four-hour job, the operator could simultaneously process other jobs on the computer. In fact, before too long, additional operators were needed to keep up with the loading of punched cards and magnetic tape, and, of course, with the very frequent task of loading the printer with paper. Operations work today can be broken down into a number of functions, many of which require as much—or more—technical training than many programming positions.

Functions[1] A data center, like a manufacturing operation, is set up primarily to produce output from given raw materials by utilizing equipment and consuming supplies. The raw materials for the computer operations department or data center are the data and input jobs to be processed. The outputs are the required telecommunication systems, reports, premium notices, bills, and so on. Only the major functions involved in converting the raw materials or input into outputs will be discussed here.

Data Conversion. Many insurance carriers have centralized data entry facilities which convert raw data, such as policy declarations pages, into machine readable form through entry of the data through a VDT or even preparation of a punched card. Like the data center as a whole, the data conversion group serves many users. Conversion time is part of the overall schedule and must be considered when scheduling a particular computer run or job, as it is also known. Unanticipated volume increases, illegible documents and poorly designed forms can drastically affect the data conversion group's ability to meet its schedule.

Input-Receipt. This function receives input data, prepares routing sheets, and expedites jobs. In addition, this area often serves as the user's liaison with the data center answering questions about job status and informing users of changes in processing schedules.

Scheduling. Scheduling is the planning and control function of the data center. The basic responsibility of the scheduling function is to provide a sequence of computer runs for a specific time period that will meet all of the deadline constraints, input availability, and task dependencies. Daily schedule revisions may be required because of system failures, reruns, emergency runs, late input, and general slippage in the run schedule. Many data centers now use computer programs to help schedule jobs by analyzing priorities, processing order, hardware requirements and resources, and prescheduled jobs.

Library. The library function, under the *librarian,* is responsible for the storage and control of tapes and disks. It is also responsible for responding to requests for tape reels and disks when the jobs are prestaged for execution. The library represents a very special inventory problem. Each of the many tapes and disks is an independently identifiable inventory item, which must be readily available and accounted for at all times. Without a workable plan for controlling these files, they can be misplaced, erroneously erased, or otherwise lost.

Machine Operation. This function is responsible for the operation of the machines that perform the processing of jobs and the production of output. It involves receiving media from the data conversion, input-receipt, and library functions, mounting tapes and disks, releasing jobs for processing by the computer, and controlling the job mix on a continual basis to ensure adherence to schedules.

Most large-scale systems have the computer in operation for more than the standard work day. Spreading the computer's work over two or three shifts enables a company to purchase a smaller computer than would be needed if all the computer work had to be done during the regular eight-hour day. Often there is a *lead operator,* also called a *shift supervisor,* for each shift. This person directs the activities of the other operators.

Output Control and Distribution. The output control part of this function involves checking the output of a computer run for completeness and quality. In the case of batch runs, this may require checking balance totals, item counts, and print quality. For data transmissions, log sheets must be checked to ensure the completeness and accuracy of the transmission. The distribution part of the function includes responsibilities for ensuring that pages are separated, carbons removed, and sprocket holes trimmed prior to the output being sent to the end user.

Insurance Agency Operations

Let us now turn from insurance company to insurance agency automation. Despite the advances of automation, computer equipment and software do not automatically fit in with an agency's operations. Automation, like a hammer, is a tool. As a tool, automation must be managed by someone who knows the system and how it will be used in the agency. This individual is the operations manager. The agency operations manager is responsible for all of the data center functions described above as they apply to the agency. When a new system is installed, certain facts about the agency must be defined to the system, client and policy information must be entered, and the general ledger, receivables and payables must be converted. Procedures for processing incoming mail and paper work may have to be revised to deemphasize the old manual filing system as the primary source of information. File backups, periodic purges of dated information (i.e., stale prospects) and day-end, month-end and year-end reporting runs must be scheduled into the agency's operations. Tape or disk copies of the system's files need to be stored safely and securely in the event a disk failure requires restoration of the system from the most recent copies. Other areas of responsibility include starting the system up, shutting it down, restarting it when the system fails, resolving problems with the system's vendor, and maintaining the supply inventory to ensure continuous operation of the system.

In a small agency, one of the staff might be assigned the responsibility for operation of the computer as an additional responsibility. In larger agencies, the function can be a full-time position.

Operations Concerns

Priorities. To be responsible for managing the data center or operations means to be constantly concerned with priorities. Since computer power, great as it might be, is always finite, work requests must be assigned priorities. The assignment of these priorities is always a rather ticklish responsibility. End users, naturally, never think any of their jobs should be given the lowest priority and yet some projects have to be given the lowest rank. Having enormous computer capacity, of course, reduces the problem of setting job priorities. Obviously, this is a costly proposition.

Processing work loads are seldom level: there are peaks and valleys over time. This is particularly true in insurance companies and agencies that have a great deal of statistical and accounting work performed once a month. Most organizations have computers large enough to take them through the expected peaks and valleys. But what if a snowstorm leads to a two-day power failure during the peak time of the month? To have enough excess computer capacity to handle every possible contingency would be an expensive luxury. But to operate the computer constantly at full capacity, without leeway for downtime, is just as costly in the long run. The solution to the problem lies in trying to strike a balance between these extremes.

Still, the manager of computer operations often receives questions of this sort, "If the new computer can execute instructions in seconds, why is my monthly report two days late?" One likely reason is the matter of setting priorities. Priorities should emanate from the top of the organization. Naturally, the top executives of the company or agency should not have to schedule computer runs for the day, but they should establish a basic framework from which daily priorities can be derived. Perhaps priorities are established properly but are not effectively communicated throughout the organization. People can usually accept delays if those delays can be predicted to some degree and they know that their managers realize and understand the problems.

Security. During the second generation and early third generation, executives liked to "show off" their computers. Computer rooms were frequently built like show cases with glass walls. The computer room, with all its ultra-modern equipment, was on display to anyone walking through the building. During the riots and civil disturbance of the late 1960s and early 1970s, some managers grew concerned that many of these showcase computer rooms were easy targets for protestors or for vandals. The glistening, antiseptic computer room was, for some, a symbol of the capitalist system. Moreover, it symbolized what was wrong with the system. Some of the fears were realized and computer facilities disrupted.

In addition to the risk of damage to the equipment, managers became sensitive to the possible loss of or damage to the data stored in the computer system. Programs and tape libraries represent large investments. Firms sought to protect their data from sabotage by frustrated employees, disgruntled former employees, and so-called "hackers" who attempt to gain access for the sheer excitement of it.

Because of these concerns, many computer rooms became restricted areas, with entry tightly controlled. Personal identification badges and locked doors became all but standard in corporate EDP areas. This heightened awareness of security was not limited to computer rooms but was conspicuously evident there. Access to data is restricted by passwords or access codes so that employees, agents, and other authorized users cannot reach data they are not intended to have. Security remains of acute importance in computer operations and is one of the major responsibilities of those charged with operations management.

Systems and Programming

Once the early programmer's functions had been divided into those of programmer and operator, the stage was set for the next division, between programming and systems analysis. Further divisions have taken place, but once again, we shall restrict ourselves to the areas of major importance.

Systems Analysts The *systems analyst* is the data processing employee charged with the responsibility of specifying the size, scope, and characteristics of programs and systems of programs. Although this is perhaps an adequate description of responsibility, it does not go very far towards telling us what the systems analyst does. Primary activities of a systems analyst include information gathering, design, specification, and follow-through.

Information Gathering. Suppose that an actuary wants a new kind of monthly report. Somone from the data processing department must determine precisely what the actuary wants before the programmer can write the program. One set of skills is needed when talking with users (interpersonal skills) and another set is needed when designing the program (technical skills). The systems analyst interacts with end users in devising programs to meet their needs but is unlikely to do the detailed programming.

During the requirements definition phase, see Exhibit 1-3, systems analysts interview end users to obtain information. The danger with this approach is that it relies heavily in the user's ability to communicate what he needs and the analyst's ability to interpret what the user is saying. Each has limited knowledge of the other's field. To some extent, each speaks a different jargon. The best results come when the analyst has a solid understanding of the company's business in addition to technical data processing knowledge.[2]

Design. Once sufficient information has been gathered, the systems analyst begins with the design of the program or system. In fact, systems analysts rarely design individual programs. They design a system and then programs within that system's context. It often takes several programs to perform what looks, to an end user, to be one function. For instance, in the case of using the computer to issue workers' compensation policies, four programs might be involved—one to rate policies, another to print policies, a third to format the data for a statistical report, and a fourth for accounting.

Specification. Once the system design has been determined, the systems analyst gives the programmer documents that describe or specify what the system must do and the manner in which it must be done. These are called the specifications and usually take the form of flowcharts, decision tables, or print layouts.

Flowcharts are made up of standard symbols that graphically show the logical, rather than the physical, flow, process, and operations of computer programs and any other process—for instance, the flow of paperwork in a department. By ignoring the computer hardware requirements, a flowchart expresses *what* an automated system will be required to do. This leaves the decision of *how* the system should be physically implemented until all of the requirements are defined. In other words, the user department's requirements determine the hardware requirements rather than the hardware being allowed to constrain the application system's capabilities.

A relatively new flowchart technique is the *data flow diagram* or DFD. As Exhibit 2-1 illustrates, the basic DFD uses just four symbols:

- A square to designate a source and/or destination of data outside the system, an agency or an agency's customer.
- An arrow to show how information moves into, around, and out of the system.
- A rectangle with rounded corners to indicate a process in the system that changes the data in some way.
- An open-ended rectangle to show a place in the process where information is stored in some way.

Decision Tables. A *decision table,* sometimes used in place of a flowchart, is a matrix which first lists the conditions that may occur, (IF customer account balance is 0; IF customer account balance is greater than 0; IF customer account balance is less than 0) and then, below, lists the actions that are to be taken (THEN go to next record; THEN go to billing routine; THEN go to refund routine). To the right of both conditions and actions are places for x's at various points on the matrix. These x's indicate which actions correspond to which conditions. Decision tables are preferable to flowcharts for programs involving complicated branching.

Print and VDT Screen Layouts. Unfortunately, computers cannot simply be told to print or display the "premiums on the left, losses on the right, and totals at the bottom." A spacing chart is used in connection with any program designed to produce reports or display information. It specifies the exact spacing to be followed in the display.

Follow-Through. This is probably the most time-consuming of all the activities of the systems analyst. Follow-through includes many things: answering the questions of the programmer; assisting in or even directing the implementation of a new system; answering the questions of users and resolving errors (bugs) in the new system; and any related tasks. The systems analyst is often a jack-of-all-trades, spending as much time maintaining and improving old systems as designing new ones.

Programmers We have already met the *programmer,* who creates and tests the instructions that the computer executes. It might seem that their work was all the same. This is true in the sense that all programmers work with detail code, or instructions, of programs. In another sense, however, programmers can be identified by the types of programs they work on. Here again we find division of labor. Primary

Exhibit 2-1
Policy Processing Data Flow Diagram

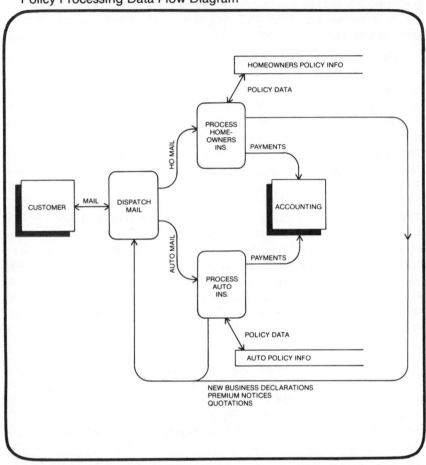

activities of a programmer include language selection, coding, debugging, testing, documentation, and maintenance.

Language Selection. Language selection is a major policy decision for data processing departments. Very few organizations use only one language. Two or three are usually used, each specifically selected as the most appropriate for the type of program to be written. However, once a particular language is chosen over others for a particular application, it tends to remain in use. Selecting a new language may mean retraining programmers or even hiring new ones. It may also mean eventually converting all existing programs.

Coding. Using the language selected by the organization, the programmer codes (or writes) a program to accomplish a data processing task. In most instances, the programmer will begin with a flow chart showing major calculation steps. Programs are seldom designed in isolation; instead, they are designed to interface with existing programs.

Debugging. Errors in programs are called *bugs* and the process of correcting them carries the now-familiar name, *debugging.* The term debugging, according to one story, originated when the vacuum tubes of the first computers had to be fumigated. Once the program has been coded, it must be converted into some medium that can be read by a computer input device. Originally, this usually meant that the written program was converted to punched cards. Now, most programmers code their programs directly on a VDT. At this point, the program is ready to be compiled. The compiler, itself a program, translates the program into machine language that the computer can internally process. Before making the translation, however, it checks for certain errors (each programming language has a syntax that must be followed by the programmer). Errors found are shown on a printout. The programmer then locates these errors and corrects them. The program can then be compiled again. This process is repeated until the compiler detects no errors. At that time the program is fully translated into machine language and stored in the computer as an object program. The precompiled (source) program is stored for use if changes are required later.

Testing. The next step is to test the program by running test data. For example, if the program is to rate automobile insurance policies, then sample policies will be converted to an input medium and run through the program. Results of the program are reviewed. Errors found at this stage are also called bugs and the debugging process continues. The success of the program may depend on the diversity, depth, and volume of the test data used to test it. The more varied the test data, the less likely that "unforeseen" problems will develop in the future. This is especially true if programs are individually tested, then tested as part of the whole system, and then put through an acceptance test by the end user as discussed in Chapter One.

Documentation. If a programmer could remember every program he or she ever wrote, the structure of every program, and the location of every instruction of the program, then there would be little need for documentation. *Documentation* is preparation of the permanent record of each program or system. It can take the form of flow charts, decision tables, narrative charts, or other written depiction. Documentation is prepared either before the program is completed, after the program is finished, or, at times, during the programming process. It is probably the least pleasurable of all of the phases of programming but the need for it is obvious. (The importance of documentation becomes apparent each time a program must be modified.)

Maintenance. All changes to a program, whether they are corrections or improvements, are called program *maintenance.* If program maintenance were unnecessary, then program documentation to a large degree would be unnecessary. Today, most major business organizations have a major investment in computer programs and large sums are spent annually to maintain them. New programs often incorporate preexisting ones or their output; properly maintained programs are an obvious benefit as new information needs emerge.

Applications Programming vis-a-vis Systems Programming. The distinction made between applications software and systems software also applies to applications programming and systems programming.

An *applications programmer* works on business problems. In the case of an insurance agency, the applications programmer works on programs related to the agency's business, such as accounts receivable, accounts current, policyholder files, and related programs. Applications programmers normally use procedure-oriented languages, although they are by no means restricted to these. The language for a given program depends on the language selection criteria mentioned earlier and the data processing department's standards concerning the use of the available computer languages for application programming.

System programmers primarily work with operating system software. This being the case, most of their work is done in symbolic language. There is a trend, however, toward the use of some higher level languages in systems software. One of the prime reasons for this is that systems programmers are scarce. Writing systems software in higher level languages qualifies many others for the field of systems programming.

Development Programming vis-a-vis Maintenance Programming. Some *shops* (the buzzword for data processing departments) organize programmers into development and maintenance staffs. Development programming is concerned with programs that are being written for the first time—either applications programs or systems programs. Operating systems software is for the most part written by the computer manufacturer or a firm that specializes in it. In contrast, applications programming offers many opportunities for development work and is generally thought to offer greater recognition. Paradoxically, though, the more development programming that is done, the greater the amount of maintenance programming that will be required in the future.

Maintenance programming includes correcting, improving, and

somtimes even overhauling existing programs and systems. Although it suffers from lower status, it is of crucial importance. It may be tolerable to fall several days behind in development (that new report for the claims department). It may not be acceptable to report delays in maintenance (correct the program that prints the claims drafts for policyholders).

Current Trends The distinctions between systems analysis and programming outlined above are valid from a conceptual point of view. In terms of specific job descriptions, however, the picture becomes increasingly blurred with time.

Historically, systems analysts were programmers who had been promoted. Gradually, recognition grew that the two jobs came about because they required different skills. Consequently, some organizations offered a career path for programmers that did not necessitate a switch to systems analysis.

Still, in terms of status, systems analysis was considered preferable to development programming, much as development programming was preferable to maintenance programming. To combat this tendency, some companies combined the two positions to create the position of *programmer analyst.*

Many companies chose to alter the structure even more dramatically by going to a project management approach. With this approach, programmers and analysts are assigned to a specific major project and remain members of that project's group for its duration. Project management does not replace the traditional structure but usually exists in addition to it. Many software projects are of sufficient complexity and duration to warrant project management.

The Structured Revolution Two common complaints often voiced by the recipients of DP services are: Why does it take so long? and When it is available, why doesn't it work right the first time? Structured methodologies or programmer productivity techniques were developed to improve the quality of new applications (i.e., reduce the number of errors), while reducing the time needed to analyze, design, program, and test them. According to Edward Yourdon, one of the leading exponents of the structured revolution, the programming productivity techniques include:

- *Structured Analysis* A formal, rigorous methodology for communicating with the user and expressing his/her needs in a concise, precise form that can be understood by user, analyst, and programmer.

- *Structured Design* A collection of guidelines and techniques to help the designer distinguish between "good" design and "bad" design.
- *Structured Programming* A philosophy of writing programs using three basic forms of programming logic.
- *Chief Programmer Teams* The concept of building a team of DP specialists around a "super programmer" who might be able to code ten to twenty times faster than the average programmer.
- *Structured Walkthroughs* The notion of "peer group reviews" in which the entire programming team "walks through" the (programming language) code produced by one of its members.[3]

The primary reason for management's interest in these techniques, as Yourdon notes, is that "the new techniques *do* work—they *do* double the productivity of the average programmer, increase the reliability of his code by an order of magnitude, and decrease the difficulty of maintenance by a factor of two to ten.[4]

Fourth Generation Languages

Fourth generation languages were discussed in Chapter 1, and should be cited again as a current trend. These languages offer two major benefits. First, they allow users to produce their own programs, thus bypassing the programmer and saving time. Second, the programmer is freed from time-consuming chores. Report programs usually do not challenge the programmer. Thus, programmers and users both are happy to see the introduction of a report writer in the organization.

Information Processing Management

Computer managers must plan, organize, lead and control activities—the traditional definition of managing. Because of computer technology, however, computer management seems to require some special competencies. There is no single job title for the computer manager. The position might be EDP manager, information systems manager, or any number of other titles.

Should the manager of data processing for an organization come from the ranks of data processors or from the ranks of management? Many would answer by saying that the computer manager should have a background in both. But this begs the question of how much of each.

During the early days of computers in business organizations, the question of who would manage the computer staff was not a burning issue. The number of programmers and operators was small. As computer systems grew, so did computer staffs. Many data processing departments became bureaucracies with hundreds of programmers, analysts, operators, keypunchers, coders, and others. Often a manager who had excelled as manager of a small programming group paled at the thought of preparing a detailed annual budget for a department of 100 people. Many organizations took care to add management expertise to the data processing effort so that the entire operation would not be run by "technical" people. Some organizations attempted to do this by installing a user-manager as the administrative head of the information processing function.

The computer manager in today's complex business and social climate is called on more and more to exhibit the characteristics of both manager and a technician.

Placement of the Computer Department To whom should the manager of the data processing function report? How "high" in the organization should the data processing manager be? In the early days of computer usage, the computer often served only one department. For example, early computer usage in the insurance industry was often restricted to certain processing functions within the accounting department. Few foresaw the tremendous and rapid increase in computer capabilities or the need to create a department just to manage this "accounting machine." As data processing increasingly became the method of producing policy and claim documents, and information and budgets reached significant levels, the DP manager was often moved to a higher position in the organization.

The data processing manager typically reports to the chief operating officer of the organization today. In insurance companies, the EDP manager is often at the same level as the heads of the underwriting, claims, and accounting departments.

Structure of Computer Management

Centralized Data Processing Management. The progression from first to second to third generation equipment reinforced the centralization of computer management. Machines grew larger in capacity and faster in processing speed. The cost per unit of information declined drastically. Computer applications and EDP budgets grew. With the increased complexity of computer technology, it made sense to have one data processing department with a staff capable of realizing the computer's potential for the rest of the company. With more and more information going into the computer, it made sense to keep control in one central place so that every department could have equal access to the information.

Decentralized Data Processing Management. The advent of minicomputers and, later, distributed data processing did not require the move to decentralized management—but these innovations allowed decentralization. With the ability to use computer power in smaller packages, some organizations decentralized the computer power to various departments. To some, the economies of scale supposedly derived from one large computer department were largely mythical because of the bureaucratic red tape associated with a large department. Users were required to fill in lengthy forms for even the simplest request. They were required to submit written statements of problems that occurred in using computer outputs. Programmers, too, often felt stifled by the paper work necessary in a large department. Where this happened, organizations have decentralized the management of information processing.

Some companies utilized the concept of distributed data processing (DDP) to decentralize some of the data processing activities without decentralizing complete control. For example, the data processing department might install a minicomputer or intelligent terminal in the actuarial department. Members of that department would then be allowed to write their own programs. Basic systems work and production would still continue at the data processing management location. In addition, any new equipment or major modifications to the existing machine would still be under the control of the data processing manager. Yet, the user department staff would have an important and significant degree of latitude with respect to their computer resource.

Challenges of Computer Management The information services manager of today's business organization faces some difficult challenges. Most of them involve keeping up with the demands of relentless change.

Keeping Up with New Products. The computer industry has always been blessed (or cursed, depending on your point of view) with a plethora of trade journals filled with announcements, advertisements, and articles about new products. These are not just little gadgets that make the computer room more showy, but are major product developments. Although it offers more options to the data processing manager, this constant stream of new products demands that the manager spend a significant amount of time keeping up with the evolution of technology. The advent of personal computers and the off-the-shelf software available for them has made the task of keeping up with new products even more difficult.

Keeping Up with Users. Users, of course, do not live in a static environment. A new rate, a new regulation, a new product—the changes can have sweeping effects on the firm's information system. A data processing manager must take the time to keep up with the other departments in the company. This responsibility cannot be delegated.

Some companies establish a group of user department managers with whom the data processing manager confers.

Keeping Up with End User Computing[5]   Personal computers have been the main driving force behind the rapid growth in end user computing. The rapid growth in interest by managers and professionals in personal computers rather than VDTs tied to host computers is due to several factors. The hardware and software for personal computers are powerful, quickly installed, relatively inexpensive, and give the user the ability to complete tasks on his/her own without having to call on the services of the DP department. In addition, response time is consistent on a PC, as opposed to the annoying variations in response time found on VDTs connected to a host computer.

Information systems management have several concerns about the growth of end user computing. Since managerial authority in large insurance firms tends to be decentralized, managers have often been free to buy microcomputers of their own choosing. The result has been a bewildering variety of personal computers in use with little or no compatibility among them for exchanging data, text, and programs. Support for end users is another concern. How can the DP department provide end users the support they require within the department's budget constraints? The support problem is made worse if there are a variety of brands and models of hardware and software. Finally, rather than reducing demands on DP, end users are asking for new DP applications and data communication services that will provide them with information they can "down load" to their PCs.

Keeping Up with Employees.   In the earlier discussion on operations, systems, and programming, it was shown that jobs in these fields are subject to a great deal of change. In some cases, jobs have been divided (programmer into operator and programmer) and in other cases combined (systems analyst and programmer into programmer analyst). Furthermore, data processing employees must be motivated, counseled, evaluated, and rewarded just like all other employees. Some of their jobs have become dull and routine: the glamour of computers is mostly nostalgic. Staff development must encompass the career needs of technical specialists and help deepen skills in communicating with users.

Computer Vendors

The term *vendors* includes hardware manufacturers and manufacturers that sell hardware and software together. When the first computers were sold, the computer itself was the entire product. In time, manufacturers added operating systems software to the computer.

Since the first generation, many other services have emerged to fill particular needs of computer buyers. One can now obtain the services of programmers without hiring them (contract programming), or obtain complete packages of programs already written.

Computer vendors range from someone with a personal lines rating system for sale to agents in his city to International Business Machines (IBM), one of the largest corporations in the world. Some vendors offer only one highly specialized service, while others offer a wide range of products and services.

Our discussion of them will be in terms of their major products or services, even though they may offer others as well. For example, although IBM is mentioned in the section on hardware vendors, this does not mean IBM sells no software.

The discussion now turns to vendors and the services they offer. This discussion will help portray the options available to satisfy data processing needs. Many organizations have purchased a particular product or service as a result of an initial inquiry by an end user. Moreover, many vendors, aware that this happens, seek to make contact with user managers. Indeed, in some cases vendors avoid going through the information processing staff as they promote their wares to end users.

Hardware Vendors   Who has not heard of IBM? The name is virtually synonymous with computers. And yet, IBM is by no means the "only game in town." Hardware vendors can be surveyed in terms of a number of classifications—by type of equipment, by size of equipment, by customer, and by additional services offered.

Type of Equipment.   Some companies produce all types of computer equipment—from the central processing unit to terminals and everything in between. Others produce only certain types of machines. For example, many companies got started in the 1960s by offering peripherals (everything but the central processing unit) that could be used with IBM computers. These were called *plug-compatibles*, referring to the fact that they could be plugged directly into IBM equipment. Some of these manufacturers achieved enviable success by specializing. They avoided the need to provide many of the services that IBM offered its customers and were therefore able to sell their products at low prices. Some of these companies, due to specialization, were able to offer superior products.

Size of Equipment.   Widespread use of minicomputers and microcomputers has been spearheaded by companies that specialize in them. For a while, minicomputer manufacturers were considered to be in a separate category from "standard" computer manufacturers. This is no longer true, since many manufacturers of large computers also offer minicomputers and now microcomputers. Other manufacturers produce only one model of a personal computer. Most hardware makers, however, tend to emphasize a particular product line over others and eventually find that IBM has become a competitor if a particular niche has become profitable.

Customer. Some hardware vendors tend to pursue a particular class of customer. Customers cannot be simply divided into two categories, scientific users and business users. Market segmentation has become more complex than this.

For instance, some manufacturers strive to reach the "sophisticated data processing user" with their "technically superior equipment." Others may cater to general business customers. Still others may seek out the "high technology" business equipment designed for such use. The approaches represent differences in the nature of the equipment as well as marketing strategies.

Services in Addition to Equipment. Some vendors will put technical personnel in the user organization on a full-time basis. In contrast, other companies sell their equipment by mail or telephone. Many of the hardware vendors that came into existence after the second generation started out by declining to offer many of the additional services provided by the established vendors. Over time, many have since added services, including contract programming, contract systems analysis, education and training, other consulting and, perhaps most significant, operating systems software. Much of the plug-compatible equipment sold today is designed to operate with IBM software and is sold without systems software.

IBM is by far the largest vendor in the computer business. IBM plays a central role because its hardware and software designs usually become the de facto industry standard. Yet this situation has been a boon rather than a bane for other vendors, since the computer market grows at a pace so astounding that not even IBM can keep up with it. However, competitors who ignore or downplay the de facto standards set by IBM do so at their own risk. To compete, IBM's competitors must undercut IBM's prices and offer better product features to make a customer forsake IBM.

Software Vendors During the 1950s, some companies began to provide contract programming services. These were often one or two person firms and many had one major client, the federal government. This came about as salaries for programmers rose well above authorized pay levels for programmers within the government. As a consequence, federal government agencies contracted a great deal of their programming work to outside firms.[6] From this origin, programming vendors expanded and offered programs and systems of programs *(software packages)* to additional customers with little incremental cost. This was the basis for what we call today the *software house.* (Language is often strange, and trade jargon even stranger, to wit: a software vendor is also called a software house; yet a hardware vendor is never called a hardware house.)

Some software houses maintain contract programming work as an integral product offering. Others will develop packages on speculation and then seek customers. Many do both. Some vendors specialize in systems software while others restrict their activities to the applications level. Again, there are many other variations.

Some software houses place major emphasis on the software needs of the insurance industry. These efforts appear beneficial to both vendors and customers. Nonetheless, some insurance executives maintain that software is best developed in-house. Some of the advantages reputed to accrue to those who purchase their applications software include saving programmers, time, and money.[7]

Saves Staff. The demand for programmers, systems analysts, and skilled DP administrators has kept well ahead of supply, bidding up the price of their labor. In addition, the maintenance of existing systems has been estimated to consume most of the programmer's time and represents as much as 70 percent of all software expenses. If a software package can be purchased, the company may not require many, if any, additional programmers. Programmers currently on the carrier's staff may be used to maintain and rebuild older systems. Within a small organization, such as an agency, purchasing software similarly means a saving in someone's time.

Saves Time. Buying software often means buying programs that have already been written, debugged, and are ready for immediate use. If the work was to be done in-house, implementation of the system would be delayed until all the programming was completed. This could mean a saving of months or even years in the case of full function commercial lines rating and policy processing systems.

Saves Money. Since the software house sells a particular system to many companies, the development cost is usually spread among them. Few, if any, agencies and brokers would be able to pay for the development of a customized agency automation system.

Arguments against the use of packaged software usually point out that some of the benefits cited above are not realized with some systems. This stands more as an argument against a particular package or against a particular vendor than as a criticism of the concept of packaged software. Another frequent objection carries greater weight—the contention that packages often do not easily fit with the procedures of the purchasing company. When this happens, the purchasing company must either modify the package or change its business practices. Excessive modification defeats the advantage of buying packaged software.

Today there is a whole spectrum of software applications available to the insurance industry. Agents can purchase complete agency management systems for multiple tasks or specific software packages to help them with specific tasks such as quotations or marketing. Insurance carriers have access to personal and commercial lines policy processing, billing, claims, management information, and agency/company interface software packages. The biggest problem facing the industry now is not deciding whether to "make or buy" but determining what the organization's business requirements are and which software package(s) comes closest to meeting them.

Other Vendors Other vendors in the computer industry—communications carriers, facilities management firms, service bureaus, remote processing operations, and time sharing firms—combine features of hardware and software vendors.

Communications Carriers. Communications carriers provide the means for computer users to establish computer networks. The presence of a remote terminal implies the presence of a communications link, usually a leased telephone line or circuit. The most obvious example is the American Telephone and Telegraph Company. Other private networks have also been established. The use of space satellites has increased the opportunity for other firms to compete in the field of data transmission. Satellite Business Systems, owned by Aetna Life and Casualty Company (40 percent) and IBM (60 percent), provides voice and data communication services to large businesses and long-distance telephone services for businesses and residences. As computer networks proliferate, this market is expected to grow in importance and in the range of services offered.

Facilities Management Firms. A facilities management arrangement usually involves the subcontracting of the entire data processing function. The facilities management firm staffs, purchases, and controls all computer equipment. Since this approach requires total reliance on one outside firm, it has not enjoyed widespread use within the insurance industry.

Service Bureaus. Service Bureaus differ from facilities management firms in that they seldom take total responsibility for the data processing function of the customer. They provide contract systems analysis, perform some data entry functions, contract programming, and actually perform the production runs. Their responsibilities include only those tasks they have agreed to take as opposed to a broad mandate to perform the entire data processing function. Insurance agencies have long been served by service bureaus that began by offering batch processing, but in some instances, now sell agency computer systems.

Remote Processing. Remote processing can be performed by a service bureau, software house, or other firm. It requires the installation of computer terminals at the customer's location. The software is provided by the vendor—usually an applications system of some sort. The responsibility of the vendor covers the proper and necessary operation of the software package and sometimes the equipment itself but seldom goes beyond this. Remote processing is of benefit when a customer wants a software package but does not want to install the package or have the problems associated with operating a computer. Remote processing stops short of facilities management since it usually leaves hardware responsibility to the customer, is limited to a particular system or set of systems to be operated, and utilizes a CPU at the vendor's site.

Timesharing. Although not as popular as they once were, timesharing firms provide service to a significant number of users. This service involves placing remote terminals at the customer site. Each customer has complete access to the computer and appears to have exclusive use of the computer. Of course, this is not actually true, but delays are minor as the computer processes work for a number of users simultaneously. Timesharing does allow the customer to do programming at a terminal. Thus, timesharing does not restrict the user to specific systems in the way remote processing does.

Others. There are still other firms offering computing and communications services similar, but not identical, to those described above. Variations are likely to continue as each firm tries to establish a unique market. Further proliferation of services and vendors is expected.

Summary End users of computer services should be informed about the options available to the data processing department. This knowledge should not be used in an attempt to usurp the responsibilities of the data processing department. Detailed examination of any product or service, and an ultimate verdict on its merit from a data processing point of view, remain the responsibility of information processing specialists. Likewise, data processing personnel should make no attempt to pass judgment on the value of computer services to users. Informed users and knowledgeable specialists can work together in assessing cost/benefits and quality consideration of alternative ways of meeting user needs.

End Users of Computers

Throughout this section on the computer people, reference has been made to the "end user." This convenient label masks issues of substance.

Growing Dependence End users continue to grow more and more dependent on computers. When an insurer puts the agents' account balances on the computer so that the monthly accounts can be computer-prepared, all future references to the account balance will require the use of the computer. Everyone is inundated with computer technology on and off the job. Personal computers are widely used in the home, at school, and at work. Advertisements expound the virtues of personal computers. Automatic teller machines (ATMs) are used to complete banking transactions. Scanners and related technology are used to process purchases in many retail stores. There is nothing in sight that appears to have any chance of reversing the trend toward increased dependence on automation.

This mounting dependence requires that end users become more knowledgeable about the computer systems that affect them as well as obtaining tools, such as the information center discussed below, to satisfy most of their information needs.

End User Computing One of the major issues senior DP and insurance executives must resolve is control over computing—who does it, what they do with it, and how.

Until the introduction of personal computers, data processing (DP) departments controlled the availability of information. With the increasing number of articles and advertisements touting the availability of technology and its ease of use, the increasing proliferation of micros and the growing number of new employees with some experience in data processing, insurance company employees increasingly believe they can participate in the information processing revolution by taking back some of the tasks historically performed by DP. This is especially true if they feel they need or can obtain the needed information faster than the DP department can provide it.

Data processing departments are often criticized for their slow response to new requests for information. In many firms, DP departments are falling farther and farther behind in satisfying new requests for information. Many DP departments face application request backlogs of a year or more. There are many reasons for this. Skilled DP employees are scarce. They have higher turnover than others in the company, which disrupts DP project schedules and budgets. Within the insurance industry changing state regulations, product and rate revisions, and one-time requests for information create a heavy maintenance workload, consuming resources that could otherwise be assigned to new application development projects. Some carriers find that the fastest way to break the maintenance log jam is to give the requesters of new information the tools to obtain the information themselves.

The objective of the *information center* is to provide a do-it-yourself environment for insurance professionals to meet many of their information requirements. The information center is not a place where employees walk in to order new applications. Complex production tasks are still channeled to the DP department where they belong, while the information center handles simple business applications. The information center provides aid to the full range or information users, helping them solve their own problems. The center may allow insurance professionals to pose questions, often a series of questions using fourth generation languages, against the large volumes of mainframe data characteristic of insurance companies. The center offers the ability to analyze options; to create and maintain manuals, reports, directories, simple memos, notes and letters; to obtain self-paced training in appropriate software and hardware tools; to generate multicolored bar and pie charts; and to develop models for presentation and evaluation of alternatives, simulating operations, and testing contingencies.

Information centers benefit insurance and DP professionals in many ways. By absorbing simple business applications and maintenance tasks, information centers can relieve the DP department of much of the crippling programming backlogs they currently face and free resources for developing complex application systems such as commercial lines policy processing and office and underwriting systems. Information centers allow DP departments to retain control of information resources, while extending DP support throughout the organization and reducing much of the friction between DP and the rest of the company. Increased self-sufficiency in data processing also helps insurance professionals accelerate the response time to their information needs while improving the quality, completeness and timeliness of that response. By learning firsthand the problems associated with the development of new computer applications, insurance professionals become more proficient at defining their requirements to the DP department and more understanding of the problems faced by the DP department during the development of complex information systems.

Telecommuting Microcomputers and advances in telecommunications have made it possible to move back office jobs out of expensive urban headquarters to the suburbs and even into an employee's home. *Telecommuting* and *electonic cottage* are two of the terms used to describe arrangements in which employees stay home all or most of the time and use a computer terminal or microcomputer to process messages, mail, assignments, and reports, and then communicate the results to the home office. Advocates cite several advantages. Time consuming and often nerve wracking trips to and from the office are avoided. Because telecommuting requires little mobility, it offers special opportunities to people whose physical handicaps make it difficult to work in a typical office. The overhead costs of providing parking lots, primary work space, and lunch rooms would also be reduced. Productivity is expected to increase because employees will work with fewer interruptions.

As is true with any new method of working, people cannot be thrown into this novel work arrangement without preparation. Managers will have to set goals and cost criteria. Managers must also establish quality standards for the work to be done criteria for selecting persons to work at home. To be productive at home, a worker must be a self starter and free of interruptions, especially from children. (Compulsive eaters will be in trouble!)

Companies implementing work-at-home programs will have to keep these workers in touch with the office by bringing them in for meetings, training, and celebrations to build and maintain the teamwork and commitment necessary for an organization's success. People like being with people and feeling they are part of, and have a career with, an organization. It is too soon to know how successful telecommuting will be in the insurance industry.

Automation Fears Employees have many misconceptions about the impact of automation on their jobs. One misconception many people have is that they will be required to have a much greater knowledge of mathematics to use computers. Actually only a basic knowledge of math is all that is needed. Another misconception is the perceived need to know a computer language and have the ability to handle difficult concepts. Automation will probably not require many workers to develop sophisticated skills. The newest software uses plain English so effectively that learning takes only a few hours. Many first-time users of computer equipment are afraid that they will not be able to develop all of the skills needed to operate the computer safely and will destroy a program or break the computer by pressing the wrong key. The latest office computers and terminals are specifically designed to require no special operating skills. In many cases playing with the keyboard for a few minutes eliminates this concern. When not concerned about having to use computers in their jobs another concern is not being selected to use computers and becoming a new class of labor, the computer illiterate. Other concerns include losing their job, and in the case of middle managers, losing status in the organization because of the loss of staff and the loss of their ability to gather and hold information. Employees facing automation for the first time often wonder if they will still be as valuable an employee as before and if they will be able to keep up with their younger colleagues.

One automation fear, the question of health hazards associated with the use of VDT equipment, is on the verge of becoming a major issue. Some states are considering legislation with provisions for transferring pregnant employees from work requiring VDTs. Unions see the health hazard issue as an aid in obtaining recognition. No conclusive evidence exists that VDTs pose health hazards to pregnant women who operate them. A National Institute for Occupational Safety and Health study concluded that radiation surveys of VDTs demonstrated that exposure to X-ray, radio-frequency, ultraviolet, and visible radiation was well below current occupational exposure standards, and, in many cases, below the detection capability of the survey instruments. The air samples showed that there were no hazardous chemical exposures.[8] Nevertheless recent reports of pregnancy problems among VDT operators in the U.S. and Canada are of concern to VDT operators and have resulted in further studies. This issue deserves further study, especially in the light of an earlier unperceived risk—asbestosis. No one wants exposure to VDT radiation to haunt corporations and society at large thirty years from now.

Fatigue is a significant issue. Fatigue—eye strain, swollen muscles, and back, arm and wrist pain—is the result of improperly designed workstations. In addition, emotional problems, anxiety, depression, and anger tend to arise when users of VDTs feel isolated from their co-workers, or feel that their work contributes less than it did under manual methods, or feel that the computer is monitoring their work. Solutions to these problems are available from the field of *ergonomics*. Ergonomics is the study of anatomical, physiological, and psychological aspects of people in their working environments. Exhibit 2-2 illustrates the ergonomic considerations of the VDT workstation.

Work Force of the Future As insurance companies and agencies attempt to trim expenses, great efforts and funding are being dedicated to the use of automation to reduce unit work costs and staff levels.

In *Sound a Clear Call*, Lawrence G. Brandon notes the "property-liability industry has not enjoyed a reputation for being 'lean' in organizational structure." Staff departments have proliferated and have been filled with people who do the work of management (i.e., planning, controlling, responding to consumer complaints, and the like). Managers, in turn, tend to deal with the daily workload—a task that should be performed by technicians.[9]

As Brandon notes, many managers really do not manage any

Exhibit 2-2
Ergonomic Considerations of a VDT Workstation*

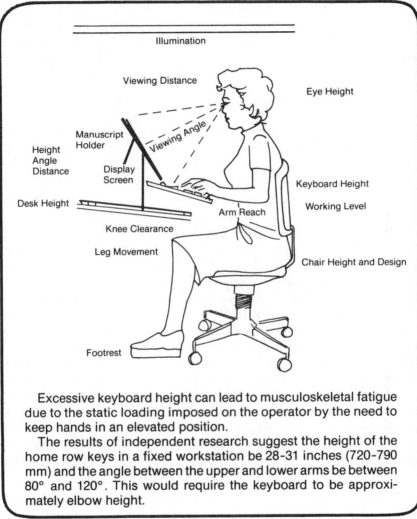

Illumination

Viewing Distance

Eye Height

Manuscript Holder

Viewing Angle

Height Angle Distance

Display Screen

Desk Height

Keyboard Height

Working Level

Arm Reach

Knee Clearance

Leg Movement

Chair Height and Design

Footrest

 Excessive keyboard height can lead to musculoskeletal fatigue due to the static loading imposed on the operator by the need to keep hands in an elevated position.
 The results of independent research suggest the height of the home row keys in a fixed workstation be 28-31 inches (720-790 mm) and the angle between the upper and lower arms be between 80° and 120°. This would require the keyboard to be approximately elbow height.

*Reprinted with permission from *Workers' Compensation Bulletin*, American Insurance Association.

longer. Already hard hit by layoffs in the last recession, middle managers will be a shrinking part of future company and agency organizations. Computers and telecommunication links will be far cheaper and more effective in building working relationships between individual working units than layers of middle managers. Overall work will be more productive, too, because the pay of individuals will be more directly related to their performance, without the middle management overhead.

Automation will also change the nature of clerical jobs. With automation, a worker is likely to progress from being the operator of a machine to being a technician with the knowledge and skill to design and control a particular job. The job of the supervisor and manager will be to facilitate the availability of information and end user computing capabilities.

INFORMATION MANAGEMENT

In this section, attention shifts from the people affected by the computer to management processes that have been affected by it. Although some of the same facts will be cited, the issues will be of a different nature. Thus far, emphasis has been on individual reactions to the widespread use of computers. The rest of the chapter will emphasize organizational reactions to the same phenomenon.

Management literature attests to the fact that management is seen as different from what it was prior to the rise of computer technology. Few management periodicals make little or no reference to the computer or to information management or management information. Some authors strongly suggest that managers must change their overall approach to management because of our automatic environment. They maintain that traditional approaches to management are outdated and unable to meet the demands placed on managers today.[10] Other authors have argued, with equal vigor, that managers do not need to change basic concepts, but need only to do what should have been done in the first place. They suggest that new attitudes are not needed by those managers who have successfully executed traditional management strategy.[11] With the opinions so divergent, it can safely be said that even if computers have not changed management, they have at least changed the way people think, talk, and write about management.

Manage the Computer or the Information?

Early in computer history, it became apparent that the computer was going to do much more than just prepare accounting statements.

Though few could have predicted the magnitude of the computer's effects, it was clear that the computer was more than some new gimmick. As the scope of data processing broadened, managers began to wonder if their responsibility was to manage the computer, or if the computer was simply the primary tool to be used in a more basic responsibility of managing information. This question did not arise overnight. On the contrary, it emerged during the several stages of computerization within organizations.

An Evolutionary Process   We will look at three aspects of the rise of the notion of information management.

Clerical Activities Changed.   As computers replaced clerical labor, new positions were created. For example, the computer department might assume a billing function from the accounting department. Previously, accounting staff members had manually prepared bills and posted amounts received in a manual billing file. With adoption of an automated system, some clerical workers could be reassigned to other positions or laid off, but the need for clerical help would not be eliminated completely by the computer system. Someone would still be needed to open the mail and enter the information into the computer through a VDT. Someone would also have to correct the information entered the previous day. Someone would also have to be sure that the computer tally of cash received equaled the actual amount of the checks before taking them to the accounting department for subsequent deposit. In short, the computer created the need for some new clerical work while it reduced the total amount. Where should these new clerical employees work? In the computer area of the data processing department, since their functions seemed more "data processing clerical" than "accounting clerical."

This absorption of nontechnical personnel subtly broadened the purview of the computer manager. As the size of keypunch or data entry and similar clerical departments grew, computer managers had to pay attention to areas other than the computer itself.

Interest in Manual Systems.   One of the primary functions of the systems analyst, as noted earlier, is to gather information on existing procedures in order to determine whether computerization is desirable and feasible. In doing this, systems analysts often become very familiar with procedures within the company. The analyst's work offers opportunity for more than computerization. For instance, the study of a problem may lead to the conclusion that computerization is not an economical remedy. Yet the systems analyst may uncover small, and perhaps some major, defects in the manual procedure. The analyst can recommend improvements that do not involve automation. This interest and involvement in manual systems extends the boundaries of computer management beyond the narrow confines of the computer.

Redundant Applications.   As applications are developed for user departments, information redundancy is likely to occur. For instance, the accounting department needs the insured's name on every policy entered into the accounting system. The claims department records all claims activity and it, too, requires that the insured's name be entered.

The insured's name is in the computer twice, once for the accounting department and once for the claims department. The insured's name is but one illustration: the cost of information redundancy is significant.

With heightened recognition of the waste in redundant data and redundant procedures, managers sought better, more efficient methods of operation. This search signaled the transition from computer management to information management.

Manage the Information There is a clear answer to the question: Manage the computer or the information? Managers are to manage the information. This places the computer in its proper role as a tool of management. This resolution does not come easily nor to everyone at the same time. But, clearly, the prevailing approach in the business world is to regard the computer as a component within the information system, and to center attention on the information.

Information: Costs and Value[12]

As the perspective shifted from computer management to information management, there was a corollary adjustment from cost-benefit analysis of the computer to a cost-benefit analysis of information. The costs and benefits are taken broadly, from the viewpoint of users as well as of top executives. There must be a way of identifying information that is worth capturing.

Cost of Information The cost of obtaining, or capturing, information, can be divided into the following five general categories.

1. Cost of the Hardware. Since the cost of the hardware is the price actually paid for purchase or lease of equipment, it is probably the easiest figure to arrive at.

2. Cost of Systems Analysis, Design, and Implementation. This includes all program development costs, from the design phase straight through to implementation.

3. Cost for Space and Environment Control Factors. This includes floor space, preparation, special temperature and humidity controls, and power control units. With large-scale computers, these costs can be significant.

4. Cost of Conversion. This category includes both the one-time cost associated with conversion from a manual procedure to a computerized procedure and the cost of upgrading or converting from one computer system to another. The conversion cost is often considerably higher than the total costs of hardware, installation, and program development.

5. Cost of Operation. This category includes the personnel, supplies, space, utilities, and other costs associated with the maintenance and operation of the information management function.

Value of Information Unlike the cost information, the value of information is extremely difficult to quantify and must be approached almost exclusively from a conceptual point of view. The value of information is based on the following:

1. Accessibility. How easily and quickly can the information be accessed? It may be a matter of seconds through a VDT, or a matter of hours through some batch method.

2. Comprehensiveness. Not how voluminous, but how comprehensive is the information in question? Does it convey meaning in its own right or only in relation to some other information?

3. Accuracy. To what degree is the information free from error? (Since no human information is infallible, an error rate, however small, is inevitable.)

4. Appropriateness. Is the information to the user's request or need?

5. Timeliness. How much time elapses from the input of information into the system until the output is available to the user? Is information available when needed for activities and decisions?

6. Clarity. How ambiguous is the information? Can the inexperienced or occasional user understand it without aid?

7. Flexibility. How flexible is the information in its use? Can it be used for more than one decision, or by more than one decision maker?

8. Verifiability. Can the information be verified easily?

9. Freedom from Bias. Has the information been free from any attempt to alter or modify, in order to support a preconceived conclusion? (If information has been "screened," its objectivity, and therefore value, has been reduced.)

10. Quantifiable. Are the facts quantified as much as possible?

Summary The foregoing analysis of cost and value components may appear theoretical and of little practical use. But it is important to recognize the need for many measures of the value of information, to recognize the complexity of information value, and to apply more than the most obvious criteria when determining that value.

Information Management Concepts

Data and Information[13] Up to this point, this text has used the terms data and information interchangeably, as they often are in common speech. Information management literature, however, takes great pains to distinguish between data and information.

Data. John Burch, Jr., and Robert Strater, Jr., have defined data this way:

> Data are raw facts in isolation which, when placed in a meaningful context by a data processing operation(s), allows inferences to be drawn.[14]

Several inferences can be drawn from this definition. First, since data are "raw" facts, they are facts which have not been refined. A $150 premium invoice or a $3,000 claim payment are examples of raw facts, of data. The second, and related consideration, is the notion that data are "isolated" from any "meaningful context." For example, the phrase, "$150 premium invoice," appearing on a computer printout with nothing else on the page, would represent a fact, but not meaningful information. But if this same phrase appeared beside Mr. John Smith's name on the "Past Due Premium Report," information would be provided.

Information. Burch and Strater define information in this way:

> *Information* is substantially different from data in that data are raw, unevaluated messages. Information is the increase in knowledge obtained by the recipient by matching proper data elements to the variables of a problem. Information is the aggregation or processing of data to provide knowledge or intelligence.[15]

The distinction between data and information suggests a defect in many information systems. That is, they can be filled with data, but provide inadequate information. It is not uncommon for some computer installations to produce reports that go unread. There are many reasons for this, but many times the data-information distinction is at the heart of the problem. The computer spews out mountains of data instead of information. The problem is usually labeled overkill: swamping the manager with data or insufficiently refined information. As a result, asking the right questions assumes central importance. The focus must be on formulating sound questions—ones that permit greater understanding and control of the organization.

Information Management and Management Information

These ostensibly synonymous terms mean quite different things.

Information Management. This term has been liberally used in this text but must now be defined. The term information management means the management of information within the organization. It refers to the manager's concern with the creation, flow, and use of information throughout the organization. For this reason, managers may speak of their responsibility to manage the firm's information system. To recapitulate a previous discussion, managers involved with computers have shifted their concept of the field from "computer management" to "information management."

Management Information. Management is the modifier in this term. Thus management information specifies a particular type of information—information used by managers or for managerial purposes. To illustrate, an insurer's information system contains many items of claims information. Some of these items, perhaps in summarized form, are useful to the persons who supervise claims activity. Other items can be regarded as technical details used by adjusters but not channeled to claims managers for their supervisory functions. The distinction between technical information and management information is based primarily on the decisions to be made on the basis of the information rather than on the kind of information. Management information reflects the need to extract from a mass of information those items that are needed by managers, the result of a process of selecting, summarizing, and presenting information needed for managerial decisions.

Systems. The term systems pervades computer and information management literature. The literature provides this definition of a system: *"A system is a set of components that interact with one another for some purpose."*[16]

The systems approach as applied to business requires that the business be analyzed as a set of interdependent elements. This system may be comprised of sub-systems which are in turn comprised of more sub-systems, and so on. In fact, the business system is a sub-system of some larger system. Using the systems approach, decisions should be reached after consideration of the ramifications, not just for the area in question, but for the system as a whole. Few people would notice if the "computer department" changed the sign on its door from "Information Management Department" to "Information Systems Management Department" but the change would imply a change in the approach taken by the department.

Contrary to common belief, the systems approach or concept did not arise in the computer field. It is more a philosophy than a science and actually has its roots in the philosophy of George Frederick Hegel (1770–1831).[17]

Management Information Systems. The management information system (MIS) has been one of the most talked about and written about subjects in the field of management over the last twenty years. Few students or even occasional readers of management periodicals would fail to recognize the initials MIS. It has a good image in some circles and an unsavory one in others. The rest of this chapter will deal primarily with the popular but elusive concept, management information systems.

One of the dilemmas facing those who seek to understand more about MIS is that there is no universally accepted definition of what one is. Logically, we might be able to modify our definition of system to say that an MIS is a set of management information components that interact with one another for some management information purpose. The following, however, is more representative of the definitions that are used in MIS literature. It describes an MIS as:

> A group of people, a set of manuals, and data processing equipment that select, store, process, and retrieve data to reduce the uncertainty in decision-making by yielding information for managers at the time they can most efficiently use it.[18]

From this definition, we can see that the ultimate purpose in using an MIS is the reduction of uncertainty—something insurance people can understand! But the reference is to a particular type of uncertainty—the type associated with making decisions. Implicit in this part of the definition is the assumption that uncertainty in decision making can and should be reduced. An MIS, therefore, can be judged on the basis of how it reduces uncertainty in management decision making. Those with insurance backgrounds will be cautious in judging an MIS since there can be a difference between perceived and actual uncertainty.[19]

The definition further states that the way an MIS reduces uncertainty in decision making is by providing information. So it is clear that an MIS is expected to yield information, not data.

The definition goes on to point out that the information must be provided when the manager can most efficiently use it.

The definition does not say that an MIS is limited to what the computer does. It does not even say that a computer is the focal point of the system. It simply mentions data processing equipment as one of the elements of the MIS. Moreover, many define the term "data processing" equipment to include other office machines. Of course, as a practical matter, a computer is normally assumed to be an integral part of any MIS.

Information System. It may seem odd to describe the general term, information system, after the more specific one, management information system. There is a reason for this, however. MIS has been discussed widely and many attempts have been made to establish its essential meaning. In fact, the term will usually appear in capital letters when in print, especially in its abbreviated form. Information system, on the other hand, always appears in lower case: the term is now considered generic. Information system is a rather imprecise term embracing the creation, processing, and use of information in the organization. The label information system usually signifies concern for the whole organization, not some small segment of it.

Summary Information management represents the attempt to manage information within organizations. Management information is only one type—although an important type—of information that must be managed. The computer is a tool with which to manage information. It is important to focus on *information*, not only on the *data* which helps to produce information.

The systems approach to information management makes it necessary to view systems as made up of parts and as parts of larger systems. This approach organizes information into interrelated systems.

The organization of management information works toward a management information system (MIS). The management of information systems, therefore, represents in one sense a subject area broader than that represented by MIS, and in another sense a more narrow one. It is broader in the sense that it is concerned with all types of information systems, not just management information systems. And it is more narrow in the sense that the few persons involved in the ongoing management of the system hardly loom large in the context of a large business organization.

MANAGING THE MANAGEMENT INFORMATION SYSTEM

Early Attempts

The initial burst of MIS literature appeared in the 1960s. The arrival of third generation computer equipment fueled the fire. Expectations were high. Normally pragmatic corporate executives became enamored with the glorious portraits of sophisticated management control systems as painted by computer manufacturers. This was also the time of the "space race" and one could watch, on the living room television set, computers controlling manned space flights. The logic seemed indisputable: if computers could fly a man to the moon, they could certainly control logistics in a business corporation.

Many large corporations established MIS departments in the 1960s. The head of MIS often reported to the chief executive or chief operating officer of the firm. The first responsibility was to define the parameters of the MIS and then bring the MIS to fruition. What information do chief executives receive? How much of it do they really need? What do they need that they are not currently getting? When does the chief executive need this information? And so on. When finished with the chief executive, the MIS designer proceeded to the next executive and started over again with the same questions. It should be apparent that this was no small task.

Implicit in most of these early attempts was the assumption that a company should have a single management information system, not a number of management information systems. In looking back, we now see the dominance of the "mainframe mentality." Computers were getting larger and faster, by leaps and bounds, and it seemed their potential was limitless. (The microcomputer revolution later changed this orientation and dampened the drive for single mammoth computer systems.) The single-system approach placed a burden on those who were supposed to turn the conceptual MIS into a functioning reality. It meant that the MIS manager had to know as much about the organization's information as the chief executive, and perhaps more. The MIS manager faced an almost impossible task. Who would teach the manager about all of this company information? The interview method, inadequate as it was, served as the primary method of MIS managers. Some managers seemed doomed to failure from the outset because they had neither the time nor the knowledge to create fully developed systems within reasonable deadlines.

The primary conclusion to be drawn from a study of the early attempts at management information systems is that they were for the most part colossal failures. There are some conclusions, however, that should not be drawn. First among these false conclusions is that some particular group was to blame for all this. Yes, top management expected a great deal; yes, computer manufacturers promised a great deal; yes, data processing managers committed a great deal; but, hindsight, not necessarily insight, suggests that they were all wrong to do so.

The second false conclusion is that every organization with a computer attempted development of a full-scale MIS. In all probability, most did not. As with many management topics, activities of large corporations tend to dominate the literature. These corporations tend to be innovative. Taking a brighter view of early attempts at management information systems, large organizations played an important role in uncovering inevitable trouble spots.

Inherent Problems in MIS

There are problems inherent in the MIS concept, but these do not necessarily destroy the usefulness of the concept. These problems may simply require that we modify our expectations of the MIS.

Practical Problems

Who Can Design? Is there any one person, or even group of people, with the skills and knowledge to design the management information system for an organization? Not likely. It would be very difficult to articulate the full gamut of information needs and time requirements for a single department or even a single job. To do so for the total information requirements of a buisness organization is obviously much more difficult.

Who Can Cost-Justify? Assuming that a total MIS could be designed for an organization, who would be qualified to analyze the system and its components in terms of cost and benefits? This is not only difficult, but sensitive ground. Even though cost of information can often be quantified, the value of information must be approached conceptually. Disagreements over the value of information are inevitable and difficult to settle. Will the MIS manager determine benefit values or will it be up to the user department manager? Cost allocation, never an exact science, is doubly difficult when the costs appear in the very different worlds of user department and central MIS department. Cost-justifying a total MIS, therefore, remains a knotty problem.

Who Can Predict? Assume that the inherent problems mentioned thus far could somehow be overcome, and that the super MIS designer had been found. The designer learned the information requirements of the organization completely and cost justified all components of the MIS. The day of implementation approached, and everyone eagerly awaited the reduction of uncertainty in decision making that their fathers had been promised in ages past. It is possible to finish the scenario—dreams were crushed when people realized that the super MIS designer could not predict the future and, when new information requirements became known, the system fell short of meeting the organization's current business requirements.

Conceptual Problems MIS springs from the "systems approach" and general systems theory which, in turn, are rooted in philosophy. What if this theory of systems is inadequate? Or what if it is erroneous in some respects? These are important questions which should be pursued, but this section will treat only MIS itself, and only one aspect of it.

The definition of MIS, stated earlier, implies that decision making will improve as more information is provided to decision makers. The stated goal of an MIS is to "reduce uncertainty in decision making . . . by yielding information for managers at the time they can most efficiently use it." Although not specifically stated, it is implied that the proponents of MIS expect reduced uncertainty to lead to better decisions. This implicit assumption is one major conceptual problem with MIS.

People make improper decisions even when all the information necessary for a proper decision is available. People who know that eating too many sweets leads to weight problems still overindulge. A wealth of information indicates that cigarette smoking is an unhealthy practice; yet many continue to smoke. Managers may have ample information indicating that their departments are grossly inefficient; yet it is not likely that managers will resign. More and better information does not necessarily improve the quality of decisions made.

Federation Instead of Monolithic[20]

Having determined the primary reasons for early MIS failures to be their monolithic nature, current exponents of MIS have adopted a "federation" approach. The idea is that early MIS attempts emphasize the massive uniformity of MIS at the expense of other equally important considerations. If organizations had not been so insistent on a single, unified management information system, the results might have been different.

The monolithic approach required that all formal information networks be interrelated by conscious design before implementation. The federation approach views the MIS as being dependent on and drawing on lower-level functional information systems. This approach does not demand that all of the functional systems be designed in conjunction with MIS.

The federation approach has a pragmatic appeal in that it retains lower-level information systems that already exist, thus making use of the existing software investment. An insurance company example will show the contrast. Assume that the company has a premium system which records all accounting and statistical information. Its claim system does the same with losses. Other major systems within the company would include an agency accounting system, which produces monthly accounts and accepts payments from the agents, a general accounting system, and a payroll system. Assume that the executives of this company want a comprehensive MIS.

Under the earlier monolithic approach, they would have begun immediately designing an MIS that would replace all these functional systems and perform many other functions as well. The federation approach, on the other hand, would attempt to incorporate existing systems into the MIS if possible, with the existing systems feeding information to the MIS. The federation approach would certainly not forbid replacing some, or even all, of those functional systems if it became profitable to do so. Implementation may be aided by another current concept, the increased emphasis on design parameters rather than on design itself.

Defining Parameters Instead of Defining the System

With the inclusion of existing functional systems in MIS, concern can be shifted from the actual design of the MIS to the establishment of its parameters. The MIS manager need not fully design all the systems to be incorporated into the MIS; he or she only needs to set forth the attributes that each system must have for inclusion with the MIS. This includes programming language standards, computer file standards, data structure standards, and other parameters.

Return to Computer

This phrase refers to the fact that the focus of MIS managers seems to have turned back slightly in the direction of the computer. This requires some explanation. As you have seen, the historical shift has been from management of computers to the management of information. Several factors contributed to this, but the basic one was that running the computer was too narrow a description of the top computer manager's responsibility. Emphasis changed to managing the information system. This proved to be too much for many top computer managers to handle. If managing the computer was too narrow an approach, then managing the whole information system was too broad an approach. This recent shift has not meant a complete return to the computer by any means. Emphasis is still on information but with the computer limitations more evident in determining MIS limitations. At present, emphasis can be said to rest somewhere between computer management and information management. In this context, the term computer-based information system (CBIS) is often heard today. The organization's MIS is allowed to grow and develop at the pace of the organization's ability to absorb these improvements. Rather than attempting to build Rome in a day, MIS planners are at work on a long-term construction project.

The Database as an MIS Tool[21, 22]

The term *database* plays a leading role in the increasing use of the computer as an MIS tool. This concept promises improved operations within the information processing area as well as fulfillment of some of the expectations of MIS proponents. It is addressed to the fundamental problems of redundant data in the computer, and to the lack of accuracy, accessibility, and control that result.

The Database A database is an organized collection of related files that contain data for the operation of an organization. The term database was traditionally associated with large computer systems, and we will use it that way here in the absence of a newer, more specific name. Confusion has been introduced by the marketing of smaller scale personal computer data management software under the inflated name of "database management" software.

In a nonautomated organization, the database is the paper files containing all of the information needed to conduct its business. In the automated firm the database resides in the memory of the computer, and more specifically, in the auxiliary storage device(s). The data in the database are collected for use by any level of management from the president of the company to a line employee. A key feature of the database concept that distinguishes it from prior function-oriented processing is that control of the database resides with one group and usually with one position referred to as the database administrator. An insurance company, for example, would have only one "corporate database," but that corporate database might be made up of several separate databases (e.g., client and policyholder databases, agency database) which in turn are made up of related files. In a rough sense, the database is a single giant data storage facility for the entire organization. The storage and retrieval systems are designed to go beyond the limits of present needs or inquiry methods. Within a few years, databases will become an essential competitive weapon. Organizations with good data base design and integration will be able to respond to strategic moves of its competitors quickly and easily. Even if an organization does not acquire or create one and then use it, its competitors will.

Database Management Objectives There are several objectives of database management.

Shareability. The various departments that submit data to the data base will be able to share in the use of data. Incoming and outgoing data are centralized, integrated, and coordinated. Users may obtain information in varying formats, but all would have access to the massive repository of data that is the database.

Availability. The marketing department may require different information on agents than is needed within the claims department. Perhaps one department requires data access by relatively low-skilled clerical employees. In another department only highly skilled technicians retrieve data. The goal of availability requires that both needs be met with minimum compromise. Computer capacity, though growing, will always be finite. Sometimes agreement will be needed on the timing of updates and procedures for revision of the data. The objective is that all data be available to those needing it when they need it.

Evolvability. This goal asks that the database be flexible enough to accommodate changes in data requirements. Although we cannot foresee the future, we can search the sky for any dark clouds before going on a picnic. In the same way, our arrangement of the data should be made with an eye towards probable future use. If properly designed, a database system will allow future retrieval in ways not envisioned when the system was created.

Integrity. Here the concern is with protecting the data in the database as well as maintaining its quality. This objective goes beyond mere accuracy of the data and includes maintenance of back-up data and protection from damage or loss. This damage or loss could be physical (equipment failure) or intangible (inaccurate updating).

The Database Administrator More than any other single person, the database administrator controls the success or failure of the database approach in an organization. He or she is responsible for the procedures that lead to realization of the objectives listed above. This includes the establishment of standards for the format of data and files within the database, selection of access methods, and arrangement of the database within the computer system. All this requires knowledge systems analysis, programming, operations management, and a thorough knowledge of the organization's data and therefore its business.

Summary The database has attained great popularity. Initial conclusions are varied; some users are well pleased, and others believe that the hardware and software manufacturers have oversold the concept. Time will reveal the verdict, but at present, database management seems to offer the greatest leverage in effectively utilizing the computer as an MIS tool.

The Future: Coping with Complexity and Competition

Complexity It is surely trite to say the future is going to be complex. The signs of that future are apparent. Jobs require more paper work than they used to. Managers of old had one constituency to please—their superiors. Today, managers have multiple constituencies, including union, subordinates, and society as a whole. Clearly, MIS can help in dealing with business complexity and multiple constituencies. However, the MIS approach is still relatively new, and care is warranted in learning from initial applications.

Competition[23,24,25] Technology has clearly become a major competitive weapon and it will be one of the key differentiating factors in the battle for market share in financial services. There are three types of technology. *Base technology* is the technology used by everyone in the industry. Many companies over invest in base technology. But no matter what they invest, it is not enough to get them anywhere competitively. *Key technology* is the technology that provides an organization with a competitive edge. What everyone should concentrate on is identifying and developing *pacing technology*—technology that will become important in the future.

Agencies and carriers can use computer-based technology to create economic advantages for themselves, keep customers "hooked" to their company, and even completely change the basis of competition. The harder the service is to emulate, the more expensive it will be for the competition to duplicate. Electronic tools for the sales and marketing staff that increase the scope and speed of price quotes and service provide another kind of advantage. By permitting the sales force to prepare complex quotes and sales illustrations on the customer's premises, portable micros not only give better support but also make the marketing and claim representatives feel more confident and deal with their "clients" more aggressively as a result.

Interface, by encouraging agents to rely increasingly on a carrier's automation systems, is an excellent example of the use of technology to hook customers. As agencies integrate interface into their operations, increased operational dependence and normal human inertia make switching to a competitor unattractive. In the ideal case, the interface will be simple to use. Over time, it should also contain a series of increasingly complex and useful features that also become so much a part of the agency's routine that the agency will have to spend a great deal to change carriers.

Technology can also change the basis of competition in industries, such as insurance, that are dominated by cost-based competition. Insurance carriers and agents can obtain strategic advantage from information systems technology through either sharp expense reductions (for example, staff reduction or the ability to grow without hiring staff) or by adding value to their products or services that will permit a change to competition based on product differentiation rather than price.

A word of caution is in order at this point. One danger with technology is that the computer cannot be viewed as the answer to all problems facing the insurance industry or any industry for that matter. The amount of time and money being put into automating insurance offices and operations must never be allowed to obscure the goal of improving the competence and professionalism of the people who design insurance products and services and those who deliver those products and services. On the flip side, those who treat technology primarily as an expense item and do not address the competitive and strategic aspects of technology are shortchanging themselves.

Although it is expensive and risky, by being the first to move down a technological learning curve, an insurer or agency can put its competitors in a position of always trying to catch up, while it makes itself a moving target by continually enhancing its original capability.

SUMMARY

Understanding how the computer is managed required a discussion of the people associated with the computer. Some positions within the company exist solely because of the computer. Other positions have changed because of the computer. The two major divisions of computer management are, on the one hand, operations, and, on the other hand, systems and programming. Computer managers are located high in the organizational hierarchy. They face great challenges as the top computer managers in their respective organizations. Keeping up to date in the computer field must be coupled with efforts to keep abreast, indeed ahead, of organizational needs.

Information management encompasses many concepts which sound similar but which, upon inspection, reveal important differences. When computer management became information management, the ramifications were many and enduring. This shift drew heavily on the "systems" approach. This approach led to the development of management information systems (MIS).

Management information systems have suffered what might be described as a roller coaster history. Their current use is tied closely to a concept called database management. This concept originated as a computer management concept but promises to provide the means for achieving some of the goals always envisioned for MIS.

The future is not clear for computers, information management, or MIS. Developments, opportunities, and challenges abound.

Chapter Notes

1. Robert Kinderlehrer, *Handbook for Data Center Management* (Wellesley, MA: Q.E.D. Information Sciences, Inc., 1979), pp. 3–18.
2. Michael D. Gantt, "Up from Computerese," *Interface: Insurance Industry* (Winter, 1978), p. 8.
3. Edward Yourdon, *How to Manage Structured Programming* (New York, NY: Yourdon Inc., 1976), p. 2.
4. Yourdon, p. 2.
5. Richard G. Canning, ed., "Coping with End User Computing," *EDP Analyzer* (February, 1984), pp. 6–7.
6. The Diebold Group, ed., *Automatic Data Processing Handbook* (New York: McGraw-Hill, 1977), pp. 5–6.
7. Michael D. Gantt, "First Buyer: Beware of Great Expectations," *Computerworld* (January 29, 1979), p. S-5.
8. National Institute for Occupational Safety and Health (NIOSH), *Potential Health Hazards of Video Display Terminals* (Cincinnati, OH: NIOSH Publication No. 81-129, 1981).
9. Lawrence G. Brandon, *Sound A Clear Call* (Malvern, PA: CPCU–Harry J. Loman Foundation, 1984), pp. 127–128.
10. Robert G. Murdick, Joel E. Ross, and James R. Claggett, *Information Systems for Modern Management*, 3rd ed. (Englewood Cliffs, NJ: Prentice-Hall, 1984), pp. 19–20.
11. John Dearden, "MIS Is a Mirage," *Harvard Business Review* (January–February 1972), p. 90.
12. John G. Burch, Jr., and Felix R. Strater, Jr., *Information Systems: Theory and Practice* (New York: John Wiley & Sons, 1974), pp. 30–35.
13. Burch and Strater, pp. 23–25.
14. Burch and Strater, pp. 23–25.
15. Burch and Strater, pp. 23–25.
16. James A. Senn, *Information Systems in Management* (Belmont, CA: Wadsworth Publishing Co., 1978), p. 46.
17. Robert G. Murdick and Joel E. Ross, *MIS in Action* (St. Paul, MN: West Publishing Co., 1975), p. 56.
18. Robert G. Murdick and Joel E. Ross, *Information Systems for Modern Management*, 2nd ed. (Englewood Cliffs, NJ: Prentice-Hall, 1975), p. 9.
19. James L. Athearn, *Risk and Insurance* (St. Paul, MN: West Publishing Co., 1977), pp. 4–5.
20. Senn, pp. 373–375.
21. Senn, pp. 384–402.
22. F. Warren McFarlan and Richard L. Noland, eds., *The Information Systems Handbook* (Homewood, IL: Dow Jones-Irwin, 1975), pp. 659–685.
23. Frank R. Orzell, "Meeting the Competitive Challenge," *ICP Insurance Software* (Summer 1984), pp. 8–9.

24. Brandon, pp. 111–112.
25. F. Warren McFarlan, "Information Technology Changes the Way You Compete," *Howard Business Review* (May–June 1984), pp. 98–101.

CHAPTER 3

Computers and Insurance

EDUCATIONAL OBJECTIVES

Describe the present and expected future use of computers in insurance companies.

Describe the present and expected future use of computers in insurance agencies.

Contrast the four general types of agency automation.

Explain agency/company interface.

Explain the present status of agency company interface and explain the obstacles to full interface.

Describe the goals and role of IIR/ACORD.

Describe the goals of IVANS and reasons why implementation has been slow.

Explain the roadblocks to the progress of automation in the insurance industry.

CHAPTER 3

Computers and Insurance

INTRODUCTION

Chapter 1 focused on the computer itself. It was viewed conceptually, physically, analytically, and historically. The discussion was restricted to the computer and its development. Chapter 2 concentrated on the people and events associated with the computer. It described some of the ways in which computers have had an effect on people and events in business, as well as ways in which people and events in business have had an effect on computers and their use. This discussion applied to most of American industry, including the insurance industry. Chapter 3 will focus on the use of computers in the insurance industry.

The chapter begins with a look at the need for computers in the typical insurance company. What are the unique requirements of an insurance company that make a large investment in computer equipment worthwhile? What can be learned from a brief review of the history of the use of computers in the insurance field? How are computers used currently? This look at computers and the insurance company will attempt to answer these and other questions.

The insurance agency will then be examined. The needs of an insurance agency are quite different from those of an insurer. Early efforts toward office automation in insurance agencies will be described, followed by a discussion of current computer activity within agencies. It should be noted that the interest of the computer industry in the insurance industry currently runs very high when the subject of agency automation and agency-company interface are discussed.

As a matter of convenience, we will use the term *agency* to include independent and exclusive agencies as well as brokerage firms. Not every organization in the insurance industry is either an insurer or an agency. Yet insurers and agencies, together, give us the major outlines of insurance industry activity. Moreover, other organizations in the industry (regulatory or statistical organizations) are in some way associated with or deal directly with insurers or agencies. These "other" organizations will be mentioned as their computer activities touch on those of insurers or agencies.

The last section of this chapter deals with topics of current interest to the insurance industry. Some observers believe that the insurance industry has a potential for computerization exceeded by few other segments of our economy. Specific attention will be given to the MIS concept and its emerging application in the insurance industry. Technological advances are expected to pave new avenues of increased automation for the industry. Such concerns as management control and privacy of information promise to present roadblocks. All things considered, there are many difficult decisions ahead as the insurance industry embraces computer power.

COMPUTERS AND THE INSURANCE COMPANY

An insurance company without a computer is like a cowboy without his horse: a rare sight indeed. To carry the analogy further, although the cowboy without a horse remains a cowboy, he is nonetheless at a distinct disadvantage when competing against cowboys with horses. This does not mean, of course, that every insurer has its own large-scale computer and has completely automated every aspect of internal processing activity. Some insurers deal with service bureaus or other data processing vendors, rather than operate their own computers. Moreover, regardless of the type of vendor used by the insurer, the level of automation varies considerably. It is necessary to analyze how these various and diverse levels of automation were achieved. What were the earliest applications "computerized" in the insurance company? What functions are currently performed by computers?

The Need

Before describing the early computer applications in insurance companies, we should specify the need for computers in the insurance company. In doing so, the approach taken is not unlike that of a systems analyst charged with the responsibility of determining the feasibility and the desirability of using the computer for certain functions within the company.

Does an insurance company need a computer? This might sound like a superfluous question, but it is the basic one every systems analyst must ask. Some organizations have found themselves in a "computer mess" after jumping into computer utilization without careful consideration of this question. For a particular insurance company, the answer to this question may vary depending on the circumstances. In general, however, we can state that the answer is yes for most insurance companies. Put simply, the computer can meet economically many of the information needs of an insurance company. The dynamic nature of the computer field must be kept in mind throughout this discussion. Answers that are hard to provide today may seem obvious tomorrow. For example, it is very common now for computers to rate and issue policies. It seems obvious that the actual rating of many, but of course not all, policies and their subsequent typing are chores better suited to computers than to talented people. This was not so obvious, however, a few years ago. Personal computers also illustrate this rapid change. We can easily see the need for them in the insurance organization of today, but would we have seen the need as clearly before PCs became an economic reality? In short, seeing the need for computers is necessarily affected by one's knowledge of computer capabilities.

An insurance company's computer needs may be divided into two categories, existing needs and developing needs. As the terms might imply, existing needs include those functions that are currently performed by insurers and would have to be performed even if computers did not exist. Developing needs are those that arise or are recognized because the computer is already in use within the insurance company.

The primary value in distinguishing between the two types of needs becomes clear with an economic analysis of potential computer applications. For existing applications, the costs and benefits are relatively easy to determine. The question then is, "Can the computer perform the function at lower expense than the current procedure?" Although a cost-benefit analysis is not always a simple procedure, at least the cost and benefit information is available for both the existing method and the computerized method. When discussing developing needs, however, the situation is changed. Since the computer is performing some new function, there is no "old" method with known attendant costs.

Existing Needs Existing needs can be subdivided into two categories, internal and external. Internal needs are within the insurance company itself—the needs for information processing that exist in the various departments of the insurer. External needs are the needs of those organizations outside of the insurer that require or request information processing. A computer fills an internal need when, for example, it provides up-to-date information on an automobile policy to an underwriter. It is filling an external requirement when, for example, it provides financial results to a state insurance department.

Internal Needs.

Underwriting. The principal line underwriting functions include selection of insureds, classification and determination of proper coverage, determination of the appropriate rate or price, and producer and policyholder service.[1] Unfortunately, underwriters are frequently unable to spend the majority of their time performing these functions. This is due primarily to the fact that performance of each of these functions, particularly the first two, is predicated on having the necessary information.

Selection of insureds obviously requires information about each insured, normally in the form of an application for insurance. A computer can be used to store this information. As time goes by, various changes occur to the insured and the policy. A computer is the ideal device for storing these changes and providing the underwriter with information about the insured for subsequent decisions concerning continuation or nonrenewal. This does not mean that all information necessary for the selection decision can be stored in the computer. The actual amount of information stored will be a function of other considerations, including the costs of currently available storage equipment.

To classify and determine proper coverage also requires immediate access to information that a computer can best provide. The particular advantage of the computer is evident when any subsequent decisions must be made on a particular applicant. To be more specific, the underwriter's handling of a policy change is simplified and speeded by access to the original classification information in the computer and available to the underwriter through a video display terminal. Renewal underwriting is also improved when the recent claim history can be compared against the overall experience of the risk since the original policy's inception, as well as the experience of other policies the insured has with the company.

The determination of the appropriate rate or price can certainly be handled by the computer for many lines of business. Of course, where the rate is established in whole or part on the basis of the underwriter's judgment, the computer is unable to perform the task. In the case of a family automobile policy, the premium is determined by the application of a formula and, therefore, the computer can be programmed to calculate it.

Producer and policyholder service provide many opportunities for computerization. Automation of clerical underwriting functions not only frees underwriting personnel for other, more responsible duties, but also reduces the need for specialized underwriting expertise at every location. Once the information contained in policy files is stored in a computer file, the policy can be underwritten anywhere, not just at the servicing branch. The ability to route risks to other offices will allow the branch to concentrate on those lines and coverages making up the bulk of its business. Unusual policies will be routed to underwriters experienced in those lines and coverages in regional and/or at the home office for processing or processing by both the branch and remote underwriters as they simultaneously look at the risk on their respective VDTs.

Claims. The claims function of the insurer is to comply with the terms of the policy by engaging in investigation, evaluation, negotiation, and settlement of claims. This overall function is the responsibility of the claims department.[2] The need for computers in this area of insurer operations is intensified by the realization that claims department personnel deal directly with policyholders and thus have a great responsibility for "customer relations."

Implicit in the responsibility of the claims department is the need for information. The person settling the claim will require information about the loss itself and will also require information about the specific terms of the policy. It is easy to overlook this need for information about the policy by assuming that this information is already known by the person handling the claim. While it is true that claims personnel usually have very specific knowledge of a given policy (for example, a homeowners policy), it is not true that every policy will have identical coverages (some have higher limits of coverage, some have broader coverages, and so on). The claims staff member, therefore, needs to know the specific coverages provided in order to determine if the loss in question is covered. the computer can fill this need for access to coverage information and make it immediately available through some sort of terminal device or portable computer. In addition computers can be used to schedule claim adjustor assignments, monitor claim and loss adjustment expenses, and even estimate the cost to repair a damaged automobile.

The claims department also needs a computer to keep records of losses that have previously occurred. This assists in estimating future losses, as well as providing claim and loss information to underwriting. Computers can be used to show frequency and severity of losses and trends over time. The computer can, for instance, identify particular geographic areas with rising claim frequency. Today's claims departments have a vital need for accurate, up-to-date, and immediately accessible information that only computers can provide.

Accounting. Perhaps the most obvious insurance company need for computers is in the accounting department. One responsibility alone—keeping track of all money coming into and leaving the company—would be extremely difficult without a computer. Imagine a room full of clerks with green eyeshades and quill pens keeping track of policyholders and producer payments. The scene probably seems ridiculous and it should. Nevertheless, it would take an army of such clerks (sans eyeshades and quill pens) to perform the same accounting functions that computers now accomplish.

The accounting department must keep track of all premium transactions. This includes the original billing and all necessary follow-ups. It also includes premium billings for changes in coverage. Additionally, all return premiums for reduced coverage or cancellations must be processed. Historically, most of these transactions were handled through the agency. The agency would bill and receive premiums from the insured and periodically remit the money to the company. Direct billing (wherein the company bills and receives the premium directly from the insured) is now common, especially in personal lines insurance. Direct billing involves even more bookkeeping work for the company accounting department and, hence, the need for computers is even greater.

Claims disbursements must also be recorded. How much money is being paid out in claims per month? How much money should be kept in the demand account? How many checks or drafts have been written but have not yet been cashed? These are the types of questions that computers can answer with particular advantage.

Marketing. Although agents certainly are involved in marketing, their needs are discussed in a later section. Here we are concerned with the insurer's part of the marketing effort, perhaps best described as sales management. The three major marketing functions are selecting segments of the available market, selecting the insurance services that will be most appealing to those market segments and most profitable to the company, and managing the producers who sell and service the market segments.[3]

Some insurance policies will be more profitable to the company than others. The company naturally wants to sell as many of the more profitable policy lines as possible. The tricky part is determining which policies are profitable, and where they are profitable, and by how much. This requires the laborious accumulation, organization, and summarization of detail for which the computer is so uniquely suited. Even where this type of analysis can be performed manually, the computer offers results far more quickly.

The sales management function of an insurer can benefit from computers in managing producers. There is a continuing need for timely information about each producer. What type of business has the producer been submitting? How much premium does the producer generate? What about the claim history and other quality aspects of a producer's business such as the reasons for rejects, cancellations, nonrenewals, and lost quotes?

The role of the computer in the marketing area is gaining increasing attention by many insurance company executives. It is not so much that the need has been ignored in the past, but that information now stored in the computer for other purposes is being channeled to sharpen the marketing effort.

Planning. Managers of insurance companies are aware of the growing potential of computers to enhance the planning process. In particular, the computer aids the analysis of the cyclical fluctuations in underwriting results that beset the insurance industry. A computer can be helpful in corporate planning since it can be used to develop a variety of possible business scenarios not feasible before. A computer model allows systematic evaluation of the effects of changes in economic and market variables on company results. Although some executives may still feel comfortable projecting the future "on the back of an envelope," most believe that use of the computer is the only way to come up with worthwhile projections.

Another need for computers in the area of planning involves the recording of goals and objectives. A project management system, existing in the form of computer software, allows an overall management plan to be constructed and disseminated in the most intricate detail. The computer could be programmed to identify performance dependencies within the organization. Other sophisticated management planning procedures including Critical Path Method (CPM) and Programmed Evaluation and Review Technique (PERT) are usually feasible only with a computer and the necessary software.

Control. With organizational objectives stored in the computer, the control process can be improved. This improvement takes place as actual results are fed into the computer, compared to objectives, and noteworthy discrepencies reported. Obviously, the computer does not perform some sophisticated function that man has never before performed, but it does provide many more computations and comparisons than are likely to exist under a manual system, allowing managers to react to and solve problems sooner.

Part of the MIS mystique is that top executives will be able to monitor all the important activities throughout the organization. Moreover, they will not have to wait until some periodic review process to determine how well lower level managers have met their objectives. The MIS, if properly constructed, will incorporate all existing systems, "observe" the ongoing performance of these subordinate systems, and report conditions that exceed predetermined tolerance.

External Needs.

Policyholders. The insurance company has an obvious need for computers in dealing with policyholders. This does not mean that computers should replace human contact. On the contrary, there seems to be little enough human contact already. But the insurer needs to provide the insured with a considerable amount of information. First of all, the insured must receive a policy from the company. A computer can prepare policies more quickly, more accurately, and at lower cost than typists can.

Direct billing would be economically impossible without the computer. As multiple and budget payment plans become more popular, the computer's role will continue to grow.

Another computer need arises from consumerism and government regulation. Regulators require that insurers provide their policyholders with information, for example, information on coverage options available.

If not required now, legislative proposals may soon require companies to show the various deductibles available and the resultant premium changes. This may, in some cases, require rating the policy a number of times to arrive at multiple premium figures.

Some have suggested the need for insureds to deal directly with the insurer's computer through some sort of video terminal, perhaps one similar to a banking terminal. Although these may useful for some limited functions, it is not likely that they will take over many insurance transactions.

Agents. The specific needs of agents are a separate topic to be covered later, but the insurer's needs with regard to agents may be examined here. The insurer needs to provide a wealth of information to the agent, such as premium and loss figures. These figures will be even more helpful to the agent if they are organized by geographic area, type of policy, and other categories. Reports of this nature are reviewed with interest, since they show how well the agent is doing from the company's point of view. Agents are eager to provide the insurer with the profitable business. Most agents are also eager to receive information from insurers on the status of outstanding claims. This includes information about the amount of the reserve established by the insurer and the exact amount of any partial or advance payment. It is important for an agent to know of all transactions between the insurance company and the agent's customers. Without timely reporting by insurers, agents lose the ability to speak knowledgeably to the policyholder.

Another demand being placed on carriers by their agents is the need for electronic interface. Agents see interface as one more way to reduce their expenses by eliminating the duplicate processing of information in both the agency and company. Interface is also viewed as the means of giving agents fast access to the claim and policy information contained on company computer files.

Associations. The bureaus and agencies that collect statistics from insurers and analyze and report the result would find it almost impossible to perform their tasks without computers. How did they survive before the age of the computer? In general, they did not collect as much information from member companies. Statistics were kept on very broad coverage categories. The demand today is for more detailed statistics.

For example, until several years ago products liability coverage was not reported as a separate coverage by statistical organizations, but was combined with other liability coverages. This was no problem until products liability claims skyrocketed and coverage became very expensive. Insurance regulators demanded specific premium and loss figures for products liability coverage alone.

Does the statistical organization need a computer because it must keep more information? Or does the statistical organization keep more information because it has a computer? There is no satisfactory, clear-cut answer to this question. But the question helps keep the information-gathering function in perspective. The need for computers in the statistical area is not simply to gather more and more information, but also to manage more effectively and economically the information already being collected.

In addition to statistical and rating organizations, there are other associations, organizations, or situations that influence the need for information management. An example is a reinsurance pool of companies. The primary insurer will be asked to provide certain statistical data to the pool. These reports are somewhat standard, requiring information already available in most companies. At other times the request will require a specific search or tally. In such cases, a computer eases the burden.

Regulators. The insurance company must cope with the ever increasing information needs of those charged with regulating the insurance industry. For instance, in recent years regulators have established pinpointed reporting requirements that enable "early warning" of threats to insurer solvency. Regardless of one's opinion as to the value of these increasing demands, they exist. As with most government activity, the trend is toward more rather than less.

Regulators, in turn, are under increasing pressure from the insurance buying public. Representatives of the public, especially consumer advocates, have become more sophisticated in their requests for insurance data. Furthermore, annual reports themselves have increased significantly in size and scope over the last ten years.

An insurance company cannot satisfy information demands with simple premium and loss totals. Insurers are asked to break these totals down by geographical areas, type of business, and even specific coverages within policies. The variations of statistical analysis are practically endless. The primary value of the computer in this context is its ability to rearrange, reclassify, resort, resummarize, and reproduce the data stored within it and to do these things accurately, speedily, and economically.

To meet their information requirements the National Association of Insurance Commissioners has added a new software program to the State Computing Network. This network is the electronic link between all state insurance departments and the insurance database housed at the NAIC's administrative office. The new software allows regulators overnight electronic access to customized reports of property and casualty insurers' financial data on a state by state basis. Reports produced include lists of leading writers of a certain line of business, calculations of guaranty fund assessments, and loss ratios by company, line, and state.

Obtaining a Competitive Edge The American economy has evolved from one centered around agriculture and then manufacturing into one dominated by service and information industries. In some industries, automation only plays a support role and can only add a modest amount to the value of a company's product. In other industries, particularly financial services, automation is at the core of competitive survival. In banking, automatic teller machines demonstrate how technology can be used to reduce expenses in an industry. The declining cost of technology involved in ATMs along with the transfer of increasingly more expensive transaction processing costs to customers have helped revolutionize the retail bank-customer relationship. Investment managers have used technology to explode money market funds from relative obscurity into a major personal investment vehicle in a very short period of time. Banking from the home via computer is likely to be common in the 1990s. Besides transferring funds between accounts, banks are likely to offer discount brokerage services and even comparative insurance shopping to their customers. ATMs could be expanded to pay bills or for account inquiry on insurance policies.

The bottom line for insurers is to avoid technological vulnerability to the strategic moves of their competitors in the financial services industry. Carriers will need to acquire the capability to develop new products and repackage old ones quickly to take advantage of emerging coverage needs and to address regional differences in the marketplace. In the future, senior management will demand that DP move quickly and flexibly to implement their strategic plans and provide them with the resources to parry those of their competitors.

Using technology to develop or maintain a competitive edge requires a large capital investment. At the same time there is a great deal of uncertainty as to the ultimate benefit of proposed projects. Insurance carriers must decide how far from the leading edge of technology they can be without losing the ability to exploit proven technology to their advantage in a timely manner.

Efficiency and Productivity Improvement Problems of inefficiency inherent in labor intense activities continue to plague all insurance companies. Today every company is being forced to cut distribution and underwriting and claims expenses from as much as 35 percent in some companies, down to the level of the most efficient direct writers, around 17 percent. Lawrence G. Brandon notes that reduction in expenses may be achieved through automation in the following areas:

- Expanded use of direct billing from personal to commercial lines.
- Increased agency automation and multiple-company interface.
- Carrier inter-departmental automation.
- Use of continuous coverage (automatically renewable) policies.
- Elimination of current areas of duplication of work between company and agency.
- Full realization of paperless operations in both companies and agencies.[4]

Some carriers are actively pursuing each one of these areas. Many others are waiting because of the resources and costs involved.

There is a great deal of emphasis on increasing productivity in the insurance industry through automation. Automation is an extremely important, possibly even an indispensable tool for carriers to use in improving the efficiency of their operations. However, automation has never proven to be the only solution to any business problem to which it has been applied. Insurance is largely a people business, and any real gains in operating efficiency must be accomplished through people properly utilizing automation.

Data processing expenditures can be a significant factor in a carrier's expense ratio. In the short term, company expense ratios may rise as a result of investments in MIS, interface, and agency automation. In the longer run, expense ratios should go down because of lower unit costs of work and the resulting ability to grow less expensively.

Early Efforts in Company Automation

As with other developments in the insurance industry, organizations went their separate ways in using computer services for managerial purposes. Although some industry organizations suggested certain approaches, companies were free to establish computer systems as they saw fit. Some companies were slow to jump on the computer systems as they saw fit. Some companies were slow to jump on the computer bandwagon and, for the most part, were vindicated in their patience. Through all this, however, there were some common experiences among those who were courageous enough to explore virgin territory. This section tells their collective story.

Policy Accounting One of the first computer applications within insurance companies was accounting for policies. Prior to computers, this function was performed on accounting machines, primarily punched card tabulating machines. For each policy, or coverage, a punched card would be produced with the information necessary for accounting and statistical functions. At the end of the month these cards would be tabulated and reports produced. As first and second generation computers became commonplace, the information captured from each policy or coverage was expanded. These accounting systems are often referred to as functional systems, since each system performed one function. That is, a premium system was designed to perform all premium processing. A loss system was designed to perform all loss processing. The programs for the premium system were entirely separate from those of the loss system.

The premium system typically collected information necessary to complete the type of business breakdowns required on annual reports. Moreover, allowance was made to collect statistics necessary for reporting to statistical organizations. Very little was done in these systems other than the accumulation and manipulation of data for the production of reports.

These systems were transaction oriented. That is to say, they were designed around the basic premium transactions of the insurance company. In contrast, most of the systems being developed today are oriented around the policy itself. These earlier systems would allow for the basic premium transactions: new business premium, renewal premium, endorsement additional premium, endorsement return premium, and cancellation premium. The system would be designed to accept, edit, and batch process these transactions. The amount of data collected by the system was scanty by today's standards.

The loss systems followed the same basic pattern as the pattern of premium systems outlined above. They were transaction oriented: claim payment total, claim payment partial, claim reserve, and so on. They were batch processed with the production of reports as their primary objective. The loss systems were seldom integrated with the premium systems because of their transaction orientation and because of the then state of the art in software design. The "systems approach" had not yet reached fruition. As time went on and interest in the "systems approach" and the total MIS developed, the idea of stand-alone, incompatible systems became repugnant to insurance systems analysts.

Because of their transaction orientation, the two systems were incompatible in nature. A premium transaction has a different nature and timing than a loss transaction. Every policy has at least one premium transaction. This is not the case with loss transaction. Current systems resolve this disparity by combining the two functions (not systems) in one overall system that is based on the policy rather than the transaction.

Rating The next major project tackled by insurer data processing departments was the automatic rating of policies. Personal lines, specifically private passenger automobile policies, were the first applications. Typically, systems were developed to rate and print personal automobile insurance policies by companies that had a large volume of business in this line. Some of these systems were referred to as "rate/write" systems. The development of rate/write systems was greatly hampered by the state-by-state variations in rating procedure.

Concurrent with the development of rating systems, many companies developed direct billing systems, or subsystems in some cases, that allowed the insured to remit the premium payment directly to the insurance company. This allowed the company to take advantage of the computer's efficiency in the handling of payments. It also provided the opportunity for earlier receipt (and use) of premium dollars. Prior to this time, the majority of premium payments were collected by the agent and then submitted in total to the company once a month.

Unfortunately, all was not smooth sailing with these early computerized systems. For most companies, direct billing provided the first experience at having computer output go directly to customers. As a result, data processing problems became customer service problems. When the computer was used in premium and loss systems, errors seldom got further than another department. The companies involved in perfecting direct billing systems had to tread fresh ground. They were inexperienced and errors were to be expected for this reason alone. Predictably, errors led to howls of "their computer is messed up." Many agents and, subsequently, many companies were scared off by computers at this time. During the 1960s and early 1970s, computer became a profane word to many people in the insurance industry. If the computer had been welcomed with open arms before, it was now going to have to prove itself.

Computer Underwriting As computer policy rating gained popularity, another concept was being propounded which, if it had merit, would fit in with the sytems architecture of computer rating and billing. This concept was to use the computer for certain underwriting functions or, in the minds of some, to use the computer as an underwriter.

Early experience led to the conclusion that performing the entire underwriting function including the acceptance or rejection of the risk was beyond the scope of the computer.[5] This conclusion solidified after several attempts by insurers to utilize the computer in personal lines underwriting. Basically, these attempts were based on the idea of assigning point values to specific factors pertinent to the risk. In the case of an automobile policy, for example, points would be assigned for traffic citations. Points were assigned for various reasons and some systems were so sophisticated that points were reduced when favorable factors were present. If the total number of points reached some predetermined figure, the application was rejected. Most companies moderated this approach by simply referring the high point applications to an underwriter who would then review them before making the final decision.

It seems clear that computer underwriting works best as an aid to the underwriter rather than as a replacement for the underwriter. With this approach, most of the time-consuming information gathering is transferred to the computer. The underwriter is left to perform that crucial function which requires more than a computer program: the decision as to whether to commit the insurer's capital to a new exposure.

Automation will not result in the relaxation of underwriting standards. However, the standards will be applied with greater uniformity. By 1990 many of the large carriers will use computers as the underwriter and policy production unit in the majority of personal lines as well as BOP type commercial lines. The major objective is to reduce or stabilize long run operating costs.

Miscellaneous Applications The applications mentioned above were not the only ones during the first stages of insurance company computerization. Insurers programmed many of the basic applications as payroll, stockholder accounting (in the stock companies), general ledger accounting, and other functions. In this regard, insurers were following trails already marked by firms in many fields. Other applications, peculiar to the insurance industry, were also developed. In many cases they were developed as related systems or subsystems to those previously discussed. These systems included bank draft control systems, agency and policyholder mailing lists, policy supplies control, installment billing control, personnel management systems, and many others.

Current Use of the Computer

The lack of software, among the other things, limited the insurance industry's early use of computers. The full potential of software lagged far behind that of hardware. Although software has not yet caught up, there have been tremendous improvements in the last ten or fifteen years. Early systems analysts and computer programmers came to work in insurance companies with little or no knowledge of the insurance business. This hampered the development of satisfactory computer systems. As these people gained more experience in insurance and as insurance people were drawn into systems analysis, improved software design resulted.

During the 1960s and early 1970s, insurance companies were not generally at the forefront of computer use. Of course, a few companies made computer innovations, but they were the exception rather than the rule. This is no longer the case. Now the insurance industry is often at the leading edge of computer technology. Some of the most elaborate and sophisticated software systems now being developed are designed by or for the insurance industry. In particular, there are now software programs for every insurance company function from policy file maintenance to agency/company interface.

Paper File Replacement As earlier systems were oriented around transactions, today's systems are oriented around the policy. The ultimate goal, at least for some, is to eliminate the paper file completely. This seems perfectly acceptable and desirable. After all, the insurance exists in the promise to pay and not in the paper itself. When speaking of eliminating the paper file, most companies restrict their efforts to the declarations page of the policy. This excludes attendant documents such as correspondence between agency and underwriter, risk survey reports, and motor vehicle records. There are definite attempts to capture key information from these documents. Before looking at these attempts, an analysis of what is involved in replacing the paper declarations page will be necessary.

One of the biggest problems in virtually every company is the fact that policy files are often hard to find. The reason is that many persons in many departments use them. The underwriting department is usually the first to receive an application and creates the file on an insured. Once the underwriters are finished with it, the file typically goes to a file department. It will stay in file until someone needs the policy—when a policy change is requested, when a claim is presented, when an accounting problem arises, or for any number of other reasons.

A file is seldom removed for only a few moments. It is usually removed for a few days. And the larger the company, the more likely it seems that the interoffice mail system will be time consuming. What does an underwriter do when the agent writes that an insured wants to add a new driver to the policy and the original policy is not in file? Without the file, the underwriter does not know what drivers and automobiles are currently covered. The underwriter cannot make a proper decision without seeing the existing file. Should the underwriter wait several days to see if the file shows up? Should the underwriter call the agent, admitting that the company file cannot be located? Or should the underwriter assume certain things about the original policy and proceed with the decision? No matter what action the underwriter takes, something is lost because the policy was unavailable. Either time is lost because the underwriter postpones the decision, or quality in the underwriter decision-making process is lost because of inaccurate or insufficient information. Obviously the same is true for the claims examiner, the accountant, and others who use the files. Productivity and often morale in the organization suffer because of this "out-of-file" problem.

The solution adopted by many companies is to replace the paper policy with a sort of computer policy. Under this approach, when either agency or company issues a policy, the key information on the policy is entered in the computer system. What is "key" information in a computer-stored policy file? The answer varies by company and system, but normally it includes such information as name and address of the insured, agency code number, policy number, coverage codes, premium and commission codes, accounting and transaction history and related data. Once this information is stored within the computer it can be accessed either by policy number, insured name, or a combination of the two. When an underwriter and a claims examiner need the policy at the same time, the computer can respond to both of them simultaneously.

As these systems become more sophisticated, they usually extract more information from the attendant documents for storage in the computer file. It is important to note that at no time is the paper file destroyed. The paper file is usually retained for legal reasons. In most cases, the paper file is kept because all of the information it contains cannot be entered into the computer system. That may change with vastly improved hardware and software technology, but at present it simply is not economical. The best example of this is correspondence between the agent and underwriter. These letters, especially if they concerned some of the subjective factors involved in the risk, could not be satisfactorily transferred to computer storage.

There has been some talk of the goal (or, perhaps, dream) of a paperless insurance company. It may be more appropriate to think of a company with less paper. The realization of either ideal seems to depend largely on progress in the development of online storage capacity of massive dimensions with commensurate reductions in storage costs, developments which should occur by 1990.

Online Access   The video display terminal (VDT), has become a common sight in insurance company offices. The price of these devices has dropped considerably since their introduction and, at each drop, they have attracted more and more purchasers.

Walking through any large insurance organization you would see VDTs at many desks and at every desk in some departments. Some of the VDTs would signify PCs used alone or in a local area network. Most of the VDTs you would see are terminals giving online access to data that resides in the main computer system. In the examples mentioned above, we assumed that the user had some means of extracting the information from the computer. This can be done with paper output, but in most cases today, access is obtained with video display terminals. Thus, instead of going to the paper file area, underwriters can type requests into the nearest VDT. In some companies, underwriters have terminals on their desks. In most installations, however, terminals are placed at strategic locations in the department, allowing all to have some access to the machine. (Terminals and personal computers are becoming more a part of an individual's work area and less an object of "community property" as the price of terminals and personal computers continues to drop.) The underwriter, having received a response on the VDT, can now determine the vital facts concerning the insured and the coverage provided in the original policy.

Both concepts, paper file replacement and online processing, have combined to attack one of the most costly and frustrating problems in internal company operations, the out-of-file condition. It would be difficult to overstress the significance of this problem and the productivity that can be gained when it is resolved.

Distributed Data Processing   The insurance industry is by no means unique in seeking the benefits promised by distributed data processing. As mentioned earlier, the organization's computer power would reside in a network of host computers, minicomputers, and personal computers. For those who were in on the development of a major online, policy-oriented system at an insurance company and also had been involved in the earlier monofunctional, transaction-oriented systems, some striking differences would be readily apparent. First is the new system's size. Before there were multiple systems; now there is one system, or, a group of closely related systems.

The system's size—although offering some initial benefits—eventually creates problems. One of the problems is that the system continues to grow after its inception. This is expected and, in most instances, desirable. First, the system grows as more and more policies are put into it. Second, it grows as it is improved. The result was often a giant, centralized system so large that modifications took undue time. Even minor changes require the services of the central computer staff. The situation affords abundant opportunity for communication problems between the many users and the programmers, analysts, and other EDP staff members.

Distributed data processing distributes computing power and the control of that power by placing intelligent terminals or minicomputers in user locations instead of VDTs or simpler devices. Like VDTs, these intelligent terminals and minicomputers have video displays, but they have more. Some have only resident storage devices with limited processing capabiilty. Others have extended processing capabilities and sizable storage areas, and features that allow users to program or otherwise modify the processing that takes place at the location. Rather than having to request system improvements and modifications from the central data processing staff, end users can program. The benefit realized depends on the nature of the programming language and the expertise available at the user locations. The proper application of this concept is not likely to see an underwriter writing or modifying programs. A better illustration is that of a larger insurer with several branch offices throughout the country. Personal computers in the branches are used to access the company's online, policy-oriented system, and can also be used to perform local computer tasks at the branch.

Software Packages

Chapter 1 cited the different types of software packages, and sketched the healthy growth of the software industry. As far as systems software is concerned, the insurance industry's requirements are essentially no different from those of any other industry. Applications software is another story.

Although there were some false starts, applications software vendors took the lead in bringing some of the concepts discussed above to insurance companies. Some insurance company data processing departments tried to innovate systems to meet the expectations of executives and users. A few companies achieved success in these efforts, but many fell short. Vendors recognized the opportunity to develop software whose high cost could be spread over many purchasers. Typically this vendor-supplied company data processing software is revised and upgraded on an ongoing basis.

Some insurers agreed with the approach of application software vendors, but have chosen to achieve the same results in slightly different ways. Rather than purchase an insurance application software package, they have purchased a database software package to manage the data required by the application software designed in-house. A database software package can be used by a company in any industry for a variety of data processing applications, while an insurance application software package, by definition, applies only to insurance companies. However, once the database software is purchased, application requirements must be defined, specifications drawn up and programs coded and tested. It is still too early to tell which of these approaches offers the greater advantages to the insurance company.

Summary

Many insurance company functions are being computerized today. This section has identified some of the major ones. Certainly, more and more lines of business are becoming computer-rated and computer-issued, although this usually takes place within the context of the online, policy-oriented systems mentioned earlier. Other functions being automated include such functions as investment accounting, functions that have no association with policies or policy transactions. Insurance companies are now at the leading edge of advances in computer technology. The future will be considered later in this chapter.

COMPUTERS AND THE INSURANCE AGENCY[6]

Insurance is an information-based industry, and agencies of all sizes rely increasingly on automated products and services to support daily operations. Furthermore, advancement of technology and the proliferation of software for microcomputers places automation within the grasp of the smallest agency.

The use of computers by agents has been and will continue to be unique. The agency's relationship with the insurer is at the center of this uniqueness. In the case of independent agencies, multiple companies complicate that relationship. While independent in one sense, the agency is also interdependent with companies for which it is in the legal position of agent. Insurance brokers may not have the legal power of agency, but they also require close, accurate, and almost constant contact with insurance carriers.

Though there are various kinds of agents and brokers, agencies will be assumed to be independent businesses representing more than one company throughout the following discussion. This approach is used for two reasons. First, concepts described for use in a multiple company environment can be modified to apply to a single company environment fairly easily. To do the reverse is not so easy. Second, the area of multiple company relationships provides the greatest challenge to computerization and is receiving the greatest attention. If the problems can be solved for these firms, the problems for single company agencies will seem simple.

The Need

All agencies perform most of all the functions described below to some extent. However, the priorities assigned to these functions will differ from agency to agency. In addition, as an agency's business environment changes over time with the addition of new product lines, sales programs, and through mergers or acquisitions, functions with a low priority today may become extremely important in the future.

Prospect Information　Prospect information is important to the overall agency sales effort. Information that is well organized and up-to-date can increase sales productivity considerably. In many cases the information required for a personal account is different from the information required for a commerical account. A personal account prospect would require information such as: date of birth, number of dependents, spouse/marital data, occupation and social security number. A commercial account, on the other hand, would require: legal entity, officers/titles, contracts, location information, fiscal year, nature of the business and special industry codes. It is important to be able to page through this information quickly to review or update remarks and call histories.

Sales Management The sales management function includes several sales support features. Marketing strategies are molded by the unique characteristics of each agency. Markets and products also vary geographically. Detailed information is required to monitor sales activities and provide sales management reports. It is also necessary to control the various sales activities by producing follow-up reports and sales statistics to compare actual results with the agency's budget and the results of prior years. Sales productivity is also a key management consideration. Information should be available for producers regarding the disposition of sales calls, hit ratios, premium/commission volume, and so on.

Sales analysis touches on one of the key issues in agency management today. Some observers contend that agents, and independent agents in particular, do not devote enough of their time to selling insurance products. It is argued that so much time is spent managing the paperwork and internal affairs of the agency that too little time is left for selling. Some agents have disputed this contention. Moreover, some argue that an agency manager should spend his or her time managing, not selling. As the computer reduces the need for human labor in the agency, the agent obtains more time for selling and managing.

Client Information Client information originates with the sale of a policy. It serves as the core of the agency's database since most of the transactions processed in the agency contain client information. An automated client information file is essentially an electronic client file cabinet. If a producer or customer service representative needs client information, there should be no need to pull a physical file. All pertinent information should be displayed on a VDT with the option to print the information on paper as needed. In addition to the detailed information about a client, agencies also need a certain amount of summary data such as the accounts receivable balance, schedule of policies, total premiums and commissions, policy history, schedule of claims and any remarks, notations and suspense information that might be necessary to fully service the client when he or she telephones or writes.

Rating The rating function is most frequently identified with the process of issuing quotations and proposals for new business, policy changes, and renewals. Agencies require the capability to issue quotations in a timely manner for all major lines of business in support of the sale effort. If the agency is fully automated, it is important that the quotation process be completely integrated into the system and not require the re-entry of information already in the system. For example, name, address and·location information should be obtained from the system's database. Similarly, the system should only require the entry of that data needed to process the quotation to reduce overall expenses if a policy is not sold. The agency needs the ability to prepare multiple quotations for the same risk using different companies, limits, coverages, and so on, without duplicating any information. In addition to printing quotations and proposals, the rating system should be able to provide agency management with information regarding frequency of quotations by company, producer, line of business, and "hit ratio" (i.e., policies written divided by quotations issued) for each company.

Policy Activity Processing The agency must process new business, policy changes, and renewals with a minimum of file pulling and duplication of information. In addition the agency should be able to issue binders and print policy documents and certificates of insurance with minimal entry of new data into the agency's system.

Claim Processing Claim processing is a very important customer service and the agency requires comprehensive claim processing functions, including an effective inquiry system, ACORD claim reports, claim histories, and status monitoring. It is important for the agency to have the ability to monitor the status of a claim until it is closed by the company. Management reports are required for control purposes. Claims management information fosters good service to clients and improves agency/company communications. Claims information may be used for marketing purposes, profitability analysis, contingency agreements, and to monitor company service (e.g., average time to close).

Word Processing Most agency correspondence with prospects, clients, and companies involves the use of form letters or modified form letters that are stored in the system. Since there is a considerable amount of repetition involved in policy processing, the agency should not be required to re-create letters, memos, and confirmations for every transaction. The word processing system should maintain a file of frequent documents that can be accessed and modified for a specific transaction as required. The agency also requires the facility to create and maintain special documents, such as proposals and risk surveys that usually require multiple revisions. The word processing system should also be capable of automatically inserting data from the agency's database into a predefined form letter.

Accounting Premium accounting and general accounting are important functions within the agency's operation. The accounting system should support all new business, endorsements, renewal and audit transactions. Since bookkeeping is often centralized within the agency operation, proper security measures are required for specific activities. For example, producers and customer service representatives require access to accounting information during the course of the business day (e.g., outstanding balances, status of accounts, and so on), but they may not need access to general ledger financial reports and summaries.

Agencies require a complete general ledger system for the production of financial reports. These reports serve as the basis of management control. An accounts receivable system is also required to control invoicing and cash receipts on both an *open item* and *balance forward* basis. The open item by invoice method permits the agency to carry forward all accounting details for each transaction. Open item by policy is also a desirable accounting method. The balance forward by account method only provides a total amount for months other than the current month. Agencies must also have the capability to monitor all direct bill transactions and to reconcile company statements: *accounts current* system for controlling payments to companies; and an *accounts payable* system. An automated checkwriting capability with automatic posting to general ledger accounts may also be required by large agencies. All accounting functions must be integrated with the management information system.

Agency/Company Interface   Agencies need to have both *batch-store-and-forward* and *interactive* interface. With batch-store-and-forward interface, once the agency representative has completed entering applications or policy changes into the agency's system for the day, the system would be instructed to transmit the application along with the other work accumulated throughout the day to the desired company. Interactive interface means that a two-way "conversation" takes place between a CRT in the agent's office and the computer in the carrier's office.

In the event that specific types of transactions cannot be transmitted electronically or if the company involved is not interfacing with the agency, the agency's system should print an application on paper for mailing to the company.

As agency/company interface comes to realization, many extraordinary benefits should accrue to the insurance industry and ultimately to policyholders. The most important benefit should be better quality insurance products. Freed of some data processing and communications chores, the agent should be able to concentrate on client needs. This might mean more detailed surveys and more comprehensive analysis for clients. These surveys and analyses could offer suggestions for better coverages, strengthened safety precautions, and application of an array of risk management techniques. This might lead to lower premiums for some clients. The hope is that agency/company interface will remove much of the nonselling burden from the agent, thus allowing more time for the agent's managerial and professional work.

An effective interface may also improve the quality of insurance pricing mechanisms through improving the quality of the available data. Because of editing at the source, errors would be easier to discover and correct, and fewer of them would get through the system and into tallies and statistical summaries. With better quality data, insurance pricing decisions can be made with a greater reliance on statistical data than seems currently to be the case.

Early Efforts to Automate Agencies

Early attempts at computer use in insurance agencies went more smoothly than the computerization of insurance companies. Perhaps the prime reason for this was that few agencies initially chose to purchase or rent a computer as their first step toward automation. Instead, many chose to utilize a service bureau—a very wise decision for most agencies.

Service bureaus had the computer experience that agencies lacked. Few agencies could afford to hire the necessary computer "expert" to program and operate the equipment. When agencies first sought to computerize functions, there were few small computers available. Most agencies simply did not need the computer power of the large systems. Moreover, those small computers that were available in the 1960s and early 1970s seldom had software available to allow the computer to perform agency functions. Agencies also did not recognize the many needs that could be met by computers. Unlike insurance companies, large clerical staffs were not present in agencies. But more importantly, the agent's concern was usually focused on the two time-consuming functions of accounts receivable and accounts payable.

Service bureaus proved adequate to the task and many agents prospered under this approach to automation. For the service bureaus involved, the applications programmed were not particularly complex. This contrasts with early applications of rating systems in insurance companies. Since agency applications were primarily of a bookkeeping or accounting nature, they were relatively easy to program and maintain. While rating logic could change with the passing of a new state law or the filing of new policy form, accounting logic was stable. Hence, once agency applications were programmed into the computer, there were seldom any major changes needed.

This does not mean that agents did not run into any problems in their early attempts at computerization. As with any new system, there were the usual problems of debugging and adaptation. Worthy of note in this regard is the discomfort caused by new forms and procedures. Many times these are attributed to the computer even though they are likely to occur with any new procedure, computer or manual.

As you might have deduced, most of this early work was batch processed. Typically, agency clerks would fill out forms which would be forwarded to the service bureau for subsequent keypunching and entry into the computer. Reports would be returned, usually on a monthly schedule. In many cases, these documents and reports traveled back and forth by mail to the service bureau. Some service bureaus specialized in agency accounting work. Others served a broad range of customers with insurance agents as only one market segment. Predictably, the service bureaus that specialized in data processing for insurance agents added more services and functions to their systems as their popularity increased.

Current Status of Agency Automation

Firms in the computer industry—both hardware and software vendors—have shown great interest in the potential market offered by insurance agencies. As has been suggested before, computerization begets computerization. According to recent estimates, there may be 38,000 independent insurance agencies that could be considered large enough to use automation.

The independent agencies, like the companies they represent, face a highly competitive market. Combined with changes in the economy, competition has helped to change agencies from organizations whose emphasis was on obtaining new business from referrals into businesses which are more marketing oriented. The desire to intensify marketing efforts has become a prime force in the decision to automate and in the selection and use of a system.

Some insurance agents are still hesitant to become involved with automation because they mistakenly believe it is necessary to understand computers or have a knowledge of computer programming to make the proper computer-related decisions. Automation is now a business issue, not a technical one. Specifying system requirements and identifying the resources to meet the agency's business objectives is a management function, and best handled by individuals with insurance and operational knowledge—not data processing knowledge. Agencies must make their automation decisions based on their organizations' particular needs and objectives.

Four basic modes of processing—batch processing, online terminal processing, in-agency minicomputer, and microcomputer—enjoy rather common use in agencies today.[7] A description of these four modes and carrier agency automation assistance programs will survey the current state of computer activity among insurance agents.

Batch Processing Though batch processing was mentioned as one of the early attempts at computerization in the agency, it remains a common and successful approach. Advantages of batch processing include small capital investment, no site preparation, limited special training, minimal agency software requirements, fast conversion, and no long-term commitment. The normally small capital investment required to begin batch processing is one of the most important advantages. Because of the small investment, many agents follow this approach for their first attempt at computerization. If it proves successful, and it often does, the agent is likely to stay with batch processing. There is no reason to convert to some other mode of processing if the system meets the agency's objectives and is cost effective. In fact, there may be additional unused capabilities of the system the agency is not even using yet that will make the system more cost effective.

A batch processing arrangement requires no site preparation within the agency since the computer is located at the service bureau. This benefit is particularly important to the many agents who have little office space. The other modes of processing usually require setting aside some significant space. Some computers also require maintenance of certain temperature and humidity conditions.

Little training is required for agency employees to make use of a batch processing service—a significant cost saver. Since the procedures are easily learned, the agency is not in the risky position of relying on one or more highly trained employees. Since batch system procedures can normally be learned in a short period of time, employees seldom have to leave the agency for training.

Since batch processing is usually limited to the most common management functions of the agency, requirements for specialized software are minimal. When special software is required, the service bureau is usually available to program for a fee. Programming is one of the important services provided by vendors.

Manual procedures can usually be converted quickly to a batch processing system. Unlike the terminal and minicomputer approaches, batch processing usually allows for simple and fast conversion of existing bookkeeping and accounting data to the computer system. The outside computer service bureau provides on-site instructions and helps implement the conversion. It should be noted that some terminal and minicomputer systems now place high emphasis on ease of conversion.

Perhaps the most significant aspect of batch processing within agencies is that it seldom demands any long-term commitment. This is especially important to the insurance agent today who confronts the lack of consensus on the best way to reach computer compatibility with the companies represented. Some agents remain with batch processing while waiting for clarifications of the interface picture.

Online Terminal Processing Earlier discussions covered the characteristics of an online terminal system. The benefits of online terminal processing for agents include limited capital investment, increased number of applicants, fast turnabout time, no long-term commitment, immediate access to data, and closeness to direct company communications.

Although normally more expensive than batch processing, online terminals offer a relatively low-cost entry into computer processing. A terminal or personal computer with communication capabilities is normally placed in the agency by a service bureau on a monthly rental basis. Whenever the agency wants to use one of the service bureau functions, a telephone call is made from the agency to the service bureau to connect the terminal or PC to the service bureau's computer.

Many agents acquire an online terminal to take advantage of the many data processing applications it makes available to them. Vendors have been quick to perform new applications which appeal to the insurance agent. For instance, premium finance contract processing can be added to the online service. With enough additional features, many agents will be able to cost-justify the online service.

A key advantage of online terminals over batch processing is the potential for reduction of errors. Service bureaus have attained a reputation for high accuracy in processing, but overall accuracy is hampered by the sequence of activities needed to correct an error. Under a batch system, entries are coded onto special forms which are, of course, gathered together and then forwarded to the vendor. If any errors are detected, they will be returned to the agency for correction. Errors must then be corrected by the agency and returned to the vendor. This can be a time-consuming process. It also leads to additional complications since accounts are not completely accurate and up-to-date. (A client may be sent a past due notice for a bill that has already been paid.) The online terminal can improve overall accuracy and timeliness since corrections are made in the agent's office. If a policy number is entered into the system and found to be incorrect for each company the agency represents, the clerk is notified immediately. Under a batch system, notification might take several days, a week, or even longer. With an online terminal the major responsibility for errors in data going into the system rests with the agency.

The fast service afforded by online terminals is significant to the insurance agent. Rather than waiting for the mail or some delivery service, the agency can, with an online terminal and attached printer, receive reports directly and immediately. Once the books of the agency have been closed, monthly processing can begin. The response time for monthly reports can be reduced from several days to several hours.

There is usually no long-term commitment associated with online terminals. Since the terminals can be rented from the vendor, cancellation is not a momentous decision. Vendors usually retain the right to the software. Because of their proprietary interest in the programs and because the programs have little custom-tailoring, vendors provide online service without a long-term agreement.

With an online terminal, the agency has immediate access to the data stored in the computer. Under the batch processing system, data available in the agency was only as current as the last report received, perhaps a month earlier. Online processing makes all data resident in the vendor's computer available for display to the terminal user. It is important to note that data is not automatically available in the exact format that the agent might desire. Programs have to be written that will allow the user to access the desired information via the terminal. In most cases, the necessary software is already available, but it is wise for the agent to ascertain the exact nature of the data stored and the formats in which this data may be retrieved.

Much more than with batch processing, online terminal processing positions the agency closer to direct communications with the companies it represents. Once employees have been trained to operate the terminal, little additional training will be required to operate a company terminal when placed in the agency. It is conceivable that, in the near future, an online terminal can be connected to both the agency's data processing vendor and one or more of the insurers represented by the agency. As we will see later in this chapter, this type of computer network is limited more by political and competitive restraints than economic and technical barriers.

In-Agency Minicomputer For the agency that has a growing level of paper work and, therefore, a growing need for the benefits of computerization, the purchase, rental, or lease of a computer seems inevitable. Even though there are some large agencies which can justify having a large-scale computer, the minicomputer meets the needs of most insurance agencies. When most large and medium-size agencies automated in the last 1970s and early 1980s in an industry-wide wave of automation, with few exceptions, they bought minicomputers. Although more expensive, the agency's own computer offers some direct advantages, including data storage on premises, greater control over data, control over costs, the ability to expand with agency growth, and direct communication linkage when available. For the large insurance agency, the issue is not whether but when to acquire an in-agency "mini." The capabilities and available benefits continue to grow dramatically. It is difficult to speak of the cost side while hardware and software continue to achieve marked improvements. Nonetheless, you can picture agency computerization as generally declining in cost. That is, a given data processing task (for example, maintaining policyholder files for 1,000 insured) is probably done at lower cost today than it was three years ago. Similarly, the price tag for an additional VDT is likely to be lower than it was three years ago. Furthermore, the mushrooming capabilities of microcomputers means that they may replace the minis of a few years ago for agency systems. In sum, for most agencies, the future is likely to include a computer as vendors achieve economies of high volume, as they compete to enhance system capabilities without corresponding increases in prices, and as they migrate all or parts of their mini-based systems to microcomputers.

Having the agency data stored on the premises offers a psychological benefit. With direct control of data and of the computer, the agency has greater opportunity to "control its own destiny." This can be an important item in the agency's computerization timetable. There are major and minor frustrations inevitably present in the vendor relationship—waiting for service is a common example. The agent cannot expect the vendor to drop everything else and work on a special request. If a minicomputer and programmer were available in the agency, an agency manager could indeed ask the programmer to stop everything else and meet the special request. This is an expensive luxury, and most agents prefer to employ a vendor's software without modification.

The second advantage is closely related to the first. The in-agency computer offers the specific advantage to the agency of having control of the data in the computer. This means that the agent is not limited in the use of that data to the routine reports and other standard output produced by the service bureau. The agency can add other systems or subsystems to those already run by the computer, if willing to assume control over the system. Having control of the data also enables the agency to modify reports and other parts of the software to better meet a particular need.

The agency also gains the benefits of being able to spread a growing volume of transactions over a fixed equipment cost. Under most batch and online terminal processing, at least part of the monthly fee is based on transaction volume. Therefore, as business increases, processing costs increase. Some allowance is usually made for economies of scale achieved by the vendor. Still, the benefits of agency growth seem to be shared, at least in part, with the vendor. The benefits are impressive when one thinks of the possible life of the minicomputer.

The in-agency computer also offers the related advantage of being able to expand as the agency grows. As the needs of the agency increase, additional peripheral equipment can be purchased to upgrade the overall capacity of the computer. With a batch system, the agent may find, after a period of time, that more system functions are needed than the particular batch system can provide. The agent may even find it necessary to change vendors to obtain additional software functions. Having a minicomputer leaves the agent free, aside from financial restraints, to improve, downgrade, or otherwise modify the hardware system at his or her own discretion. Above all this leads to a computer system that can be tailored to at a cost.

Having a computer positions the agency nearer to achievement of direct communications link with the companies represented as such links become economically feasible. The minicomputer, in fact, may offer an even less complicated hook-up than does the on-line terminal. No third stage would be involved in the network as would be the case with an online terminal supplied by a vendor. Nevertheless, this advantage is predicated on using a minicomputer system that will be compatible with the communications network provided. As yet, determination of this compatibility is not easy.

Microcomputers The microcomputer revolution brought pronounced change to agency automation. At the beginning of the 1980s, the dominant agency systems were minicomputer-based. As noted above, they had succeeded in integrating most of the information processing needs of the agency. They maintained policyholder records, performed financial accounting, created management reports, and did a great many other data processing tasks with near-perfect integration. There emerged the image of a holy grail—an agency system that did it all and did it all at once. That ideal was ever elusive but remarkably persistent. The microcomputer explosion brought an end to that crusade. Instead of a total system, the new look of the automated agency is that of a number of computers. In addition to its major computer (mini or micro), with a number of terminals, the typical agency might have one or more micros dedicated to specific tasks or functions such as for a specialty line unit or a telemarketing unit. Fourth generation languages and electronic spreadsheets are providing agency principals and producers with the ability to ask "what if" questions of the data contained within the agency's computer systems. Large agencies and brokerage firms will eventually interconnect their mini and microcomputer systems and the data they contain with local area networks (LANs). In the future, LANs will be as common in large or multi-office production organizations as they will be in the offices of the carriers they represent.

Agency Automation Assistance Programs

The late 1970s and early 1980s saw automation sweep through the ranks of insurance agencies. Many large- and medium-sized agencies obtained computer systems. Typically, these systems were complete hardware/software packages acquired from vendors. The impetus came from agents themselves and from enterprising vendors. At least at the start, insurance companies watched from a distance and rarely played a direct role in the automation of the agency force.

This picture changed drastically as insurance companies became deeply involved in the process of automating insurance agencies. It was not surprising that the direct writers oversaw the automation of their agents. The more notable turn of events was a rush of insurers into direct involvement in the automation of independent agents. Insurers changed from onlookers to committed players. They competed vigorously against one another in offering assistance for agency automation and interface connections—so vigorously, in fact, that the activity could be described as a race to place automation equipment in exchange for premium commitments. Their motivation was not simply the desire to develop efficient data exchange interface. Equally important to most insurers was the desire to strengthen (or protect) relationships with key agencies, which usually meant the insurers' larger agencies.

Some insurers became, in effect, vendors of computer systems to agencies. Some few insurers purchased system vendors and others joined consortiums to achieve the same result. Some carriers offered extensive technical help and some offered generous financial assistance to selected agencies to aid their automation. Companies offered direct electronic hookup (interface) to reinforce their bonds with key agencies.

The automation financing programs offered by insurers provide agents with an agency automation system or microcomputer with rating software or a basic agency system in return for a premium commitment. The premium commitment is usually expressed in terms of the number of dollars of premium for each dollar of the system's cost. The ratios range from 6 to 1 to 20 or more to 1 for periods of one to three years. Other programs are based on specified premium production goals and policies in force. The danger of these programs is the potential for development of adversary relationships between the carriers and their agents if the agent is unable to meet production goals because of the carrier's uncompetitive products, pricing, or service.

Carriers have advanced a number of qualitative reasons for acquiring an ownership interest in one or more agency automation vendors. These carriers have an automated system they can recommend with confidence to their agents without being dependent on outside sources, that may or may not be reliable over the long term. Vendor owners have access to new technological developments, such as the introduction of micros for smaller agencies. They also have their "foot in the door" with at least one vendor and will not have to stand in line when it becomes time to implement agency/company interface. From an agent's perspective vendor ownership by a carrier provides the financial stability and capitalization needed to support continued enhancements, problem resolution and development of interface capabilities.

Other carriers have consciously avoided ownership of automation vendors. In designing agency automation financing programs and developing agency/company interface, these carriers believe they must avoid becoming "locked-in" to one vendor in a way which might exclude some of their agents. They emphasize the idea that there is no system available today that can meet the automation needs of every agent. These carriers do not believe consortiums offer, and cannot promise them, a satisfactory return on investment because of the limited number of agencies capable of purchasing a full function agency automation system. They are also concerned about the vendor's ability to maintain the software in a fast-changing technological world. Rather than take an equity position in a vendor, these carriers have chosen to direct more of their expenditures on automating their internal operations to hasten and expand interface.

AGENCY/COMPANY INTERFACE

Meaning

One of the most confusing terms in the industry today is "agency/company interface." Agency/company interface has been defined by IIR/ACORD as the replacement of some portion of existing mail and telephone communications among agents and companies with two-way electronic communications directly between an agency computer system and multiple insurance company computers or through a network, without human intervention, unless human judgment is required.

True interface, illustrated in Exhibit 3-1, allows entry of data once, usually in the agency, and eliminates the inefficient duplication of paper and effort in the processing of client, policy and loss information by the agency and its companies. Batch-store-and-forward interface provides true interface because it connects an agency *system* (not a separate terminal) to a company computer. Interactive interface between agency computer and company computer is also true interface if the agency computer is part of its overall data processing system and not a stand alone device. Unfortunately, the current status of agency/company interface is often misunderstood, causing many in the insurance industry to believe it is much closer to reality than is true. Probably less than 5 percent of all information exchanged between independent insurance agencies and the companies they represent was transmitted electronically between computers in 1985.

Company Terminal Interface

Exhibit 3-2 illustrates that the most common form of what is known as interface today is the "company terminal"—a remote terminal connected to a computer located in a carrier's home or branch office. The company terminal is the easiest form of interface for carriers to establish. In some cases the agency can use its own system's terminals, rather than the carrier's, to access the insurance company's computer system. Exhibit 3-3 illustrates the modified company terminal interface approach. In either case, the agency can process quotes and inquire against policy and claim information, but the information is not entered into the agency in-house system unless it is re-entered separately. In addition to duplicate data entry, training, on an ongoing basis, is required to keep agency personnel up to date as new system features are added or new employees are hired. Since each insurer's on-line system is unique, the agency must maintain operating manuals for each line of business and for each carrier providing the agency with a company terminal interface capability. In the past, company terminals represented an allegiance to a company and an exhibition of technology. Today company terminals are being replaced by personal computers which can function as company terminals while providing the additional benefits of a microcomputer or an additional terminal connected to the agency's mini, when they are not needed to communicate with a carrier.

There have been some "true" interface connections between selected agency and company systems. The special software programs necessary to upgrade these agency systems to communicate with a particular company were developed by the automation vendor under contract to the insurance company. While the companies and agencies participating in these early efforts have gained invaluable experience, there are disadvantages associated with this approach. These special interface software programs usually limit the agency to the communication of personal lines applications and first notice of loss information. The customized interface software programs restrict the agency's interface ability to only those carriers providing the proprietary

Exhibit 3-1
True Interface

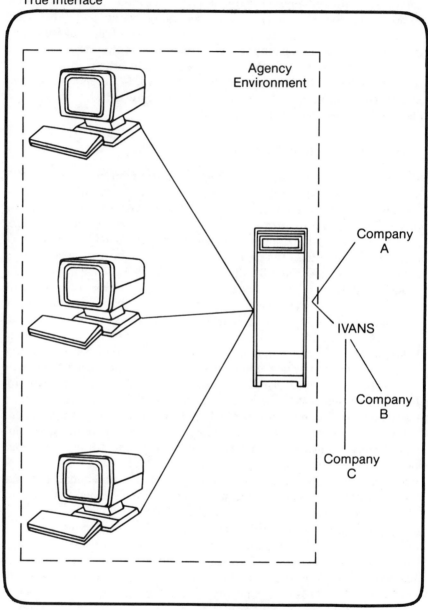

interface software. When the agency changes computer systems or vendors, it might find that the interface programs they were using on their old system cannot be used or are not available on their new one.

Exhibit 3-2
Company Terminal Interface

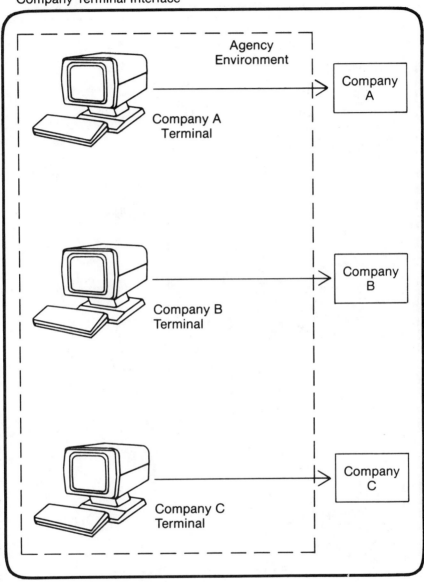

From a company's standpoint, the task of adding interface with different vendors represents a slow process of negotiation and software development, perhaps even slower if the automation vendor is owned by a competitor. There is also the long-term, high cost of software

Exhibit 3-3
Modified Company Terminal Interface

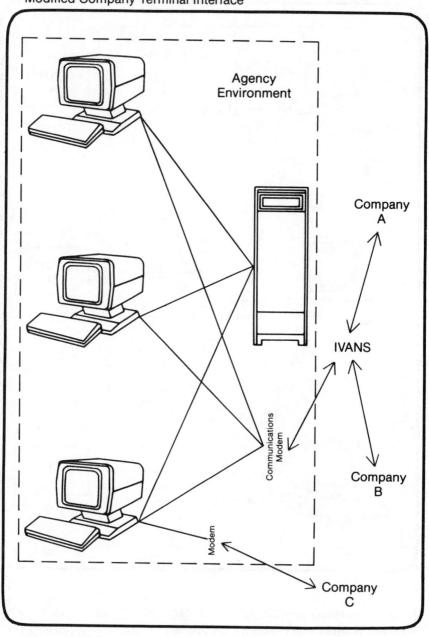

development and maintenance associated with this approach to interface.

Customized interface works very well for the direct writers with their one-to-one relationship between company and agent. The prospect of hundreds of insurance companies attempting to achieve such a link with each of over 100 agency computer systems is impractical, if not impossible. Estimates of the costs would be staggering. The only alternative is the development and acceptance of standards for the transmission of information among agencies and companies, a challenge that can also be called staggering.

Obstacles to Full Interface

The fact is that a full-scale "true" interface capability between agencies and their companies is many years away. Not only must all agencies acquire some type of automation capability, but companies must expand their automation capabilities from personal lines to commercial lines processing and must attain or approach the status of the fully automated or "paperless" office. Uniform standards must be established for both the way the information is organized and the form in which it is transmitted between company and agency computers. The IIR/ACORD is coordinating the time-consuming, complex and expensive process of developing standards. Once standards are developed, agency system vendors and companies will need to modify their systems or develop conversion programs to reformat standard information to the vendor system and company system requirements.

In addition to the matter of standards, there are data entry, operational, and expense issues that must be resolved before interface can be successfully achieved. The manner in which they are resolved will determine the competitive differences in interface capabilities among carriers. For interface to produce a more efficient insurance process, companies and agencies must determine anew what insurance functions are best handled in the agency and what functions are best handled in the carrier's office.

The most cost-effective location for the data entry function is in the agency. There are two types of data entry arrangements: one using on-line interactive or company terminal systems and the other using batch-stored-and-forward processing. Errors will always occur during the entry of data. With an on-line interactive company terminal system, the agency can correct errors as they occur during data entry. However, company terminal data entry results in redundant processing. Data is entered by the agency once for the carrier's on-line system and then again to update the agency's own information system. Company terminal interface systems are 10 to 20 times more expensive than batch transmission systems. The cost advantage of batch interface processing is offset by the limited ability to edit and check the agent's data at the time it is being entered in the system. The end result could be a greater volume of communications back and forth between the company and agency to correct mistakes before the data can be processed by the company.

Another aspect of the data entry issue is the synchronization of data among company and agency automation systems. Much of the information on clients, policies, and claims already exists or will exist in automation systems of both agency and carrier. It will be some time before standards defining the data to be returned to the agency from carriers (policy numbers, rates, premium, expiration dates, status information, and so on) are developed, since agency to carrier interface is the primary thrust of standards activity today. Until such standards are available, the manual updating of information on an agency's system must be handled with care to ensure that incorrect information is not sent to a company when the agency creates an endorsement transaction.

The ongoing operation of agency/company interface poses problems. System failures always have and always will occur in the agent's system, the telecommunications network or the company system. The remedy requires the development of complex error handling, error recovery, and system restart procedures. Software changes made by carriers or agency automation vendors will have to be thoroughly tested and coordinated so that interface facilities do not fail or cause erroneous results. Another issue is the divergence in standard implementation procedures among owners of an agency automation system. Agency A may have the latest version of all IIR standards, while Agency B has the current version for personal lines and a prior version for commercial lines. In effect, communication to a company must be preceded by an agency interface status report.

There are a number of costs associated with agency/company interface. These costs include communication hardware and software, memory and possibly terminal enhancements to the agent's system and the cost of the communication line from the agency's modem to the network or directly to the carrier. There will also be charges for actual network usage, as well as the storage of data within the network prior to its retrieval by a company or an agency.

Some agents believe there is an additional cost involved in interface, that of taking over the data entry function for the company. This is an important issue in a pure company terminal arrangement for, you may recall, the agent must re-enter the data a second time into its own system for agency use. In true interface the agency will capture client, policy and loss information on a daily basis to maintain its own automated files. With little additional effort other than the entry of unique carrier underwriting and rating data, the agency will generate the electronic documents for transmission to its companies from the data contained in its system. Some services and products (rating software and telecommunication or network usage costs) may be considered a necessary business expense and be absorbed by the carriers. The allocation of other costs (automation and interface hardware and software benefiting the agency and all of its carriers) among a company and its agents will more than likely be handled on the basis of volume commitments.

At this writing, agency/company interface should still be considered experimental, with most of the acitivity taking place in the company terminal mode. However, even though the return on carrier investment in agency/company interface is low and the available functions are limited, tremendous emphasis is being placed on eventual interface activity by many carrier marketing departments. Their reason for this approach is that they are both hopeful and fearful that their key agents will limit the companies they represent to those with interface capabilities. In only a few cases can the agent currently key data into a terminal and have it simultaneously reach the company's terminal and update the agent's own in-house automation system; in most situations the operation must be repeated. Regardless of how basic an interface capability is, those agents with some interface capability perceive that they are currently interfacing with one or more of their carriers' computers. The carriers' marketing representatives are eager to support the oversimplification that "we have interface" because from a competitive standpoint, this perception is more important than the reality of the carriers' current interface capabilities.

IIR/ACORD

Evolution

The Insurance Institute for Research (IIR) was formed in 1978 to address the issue of insurance industry automation standardization. The founding participants were the Independent Insurance Agents of America's EPIC, Electronic Process Implementation Committee, and twenty major property/liability insurance companies. The Agency-Company Operations Research and Development Corporation, ACORD, was organized in 1970 as the result of activities of the Independent Insurance Agents and Brokers Association of California. After its formation, ACORD successfully introduced numerous standard ACORD forms and procedure guides. The nearly 100,000,000 ACORD forms used each year currently provide the basis of the communication standards for agency/company interface. Realizing the interdependence of paper and electronic standards, the IIR and ACORD merged in January, 1983, forming IIR/ACORD, a non-profit corporation. From its creation, the IIR has concentrated its energy around three principal goals: (1) to help the agency and brokerage side of the industry with automation; (2) to help the insurance companies develop their internal systems to allow interface with agency automation by means of standardized transactions; and (3) to examine the needs for and feasibility of a physical telecommunications network facility to link the computers of agencies and companies.

Standards

The IIR/ACORD effort to establish data processing standards is of sweeping significance to the insurance industry. Using existing ACORD paper documents as a starting point, electronic transaction formats are defined. That is, there are standardized requirements for the sequence of each piece of data and the way each is expressed, e.g., insured vehicle. Through the development of standards, the IIR/ACORD is attempting to establish a common framework for interface software development. The primary objective of this program is to develop a communications procedure and the information formats for agency/company communications.

Despite the unquestioned gains that result from the IIR/ACORD effort, interface will not completely standardize the industry. There will always be different ways of doing the same thing. With standards implemented, 70 to 80 percent of company information will be captured, but the other 20 to 30 percent will be specialized carrier underwriting and rating data. The unique carrier information will be handled individually for each agency automation vendor or through the reduction of extraneous underwriting data requirements by the carriers.

IIR/ACORD has been very successful in meeting its objectives. It's agency automation guide and hotline service were designed to help agents apply computer technology, as well as assess its value, to their business. The IIR/ACORD published standards for the transmission protocol, or electronic envelope, which contains identifying information for both the sender and recipient of the transmission. Published standards for the contents of the electronic envelope include homeowners and business auto new business aplications, electronic memos, and the definition of print images. Many more standards are under development. The IIR's third objective, conduct of a network feasibility study, resulted in the creation of the *Insurance Value Added Network Services* or IVANS.

IVANS

Evolution

In 1981, the IIR created an "ad hoc" committee to explore the feasibility of an industrywide telecommunications network. Working with a consultant, the committee developed a proposal which was distributed to a number of vendors offering networking solutions. The IBM Information Network, IBM/IN, was eventually chosen to provide the telecommunications services. The committee also recommended that a separate organization or company be formed to manage the industrywide network. In January, 1983, IVANS came into existence to furnish a property and liability industry telecommunications facility.

IVANS is a nonprofit corporation, owned and operated by its members. It is charged with the responsibility of satisfying the data transmission needs of its member companies and the agents with whom they do business. As the management entity, IVANS assures the network services provided by IBM/IN meet its members' requirements. By representing its members as a single entity, IVANS is able to make its members beneficiaries of substantial volume discounts. In addition, by acting collectively, IVANS members will be able to exercise significant commercial persuasion in having IBM/IN build insurance-oriented services into its network to fit their needs.

There are three classes of IVANS memberships. Class A members are property and liability companies who pay for all services, which they and their agents use. Class A members are eligible for a seat on the IVANS board of directors. Class B members are subscribers, rating and credit bureaus and property valuation services, among others. Class B members are also directly billed for use of IVANS services but do not sit on the board of directors. Agents are Class C members and will not be directly billed for the IVANS services they use. Agent associations are represented on the board of directors.

Value Added Services

In addition to providing telecommunication capabilities, IVANS intends to offer other *value added services.* In order to understand the meaning of value added services it is important to understand what a data network provides.

A data network functions very much like a (voice) telephone network. It provides the medium for an agency computer equipped with the proper communication hardware and software to interface (send/receive) data with other interconnected computers at multiple locations. Usage charges are normally based on the "connect time" that a computer is tied or linked into a network, the number of characters transmitted, and the value added functions utilized. Traditionally, value added carriers such as IVANS and IBM Information Network (IBM/IN) lease underlying transmission facilities from AT&T and other common carriers.

IVANS will add value to basic telephone services by offering speed, code, protocol (communication standards) conversions, and other functions to provide users with enhanced data communication services. In other words, IVANS permits otherwise incompatible terminals and computers to communicate with one another and ensures the integrity of data transmission by means of sophisticated error detection and correction techniques. IVANS offers several other value added services.

The key value added feature of IVANS is batch-store-and-forward communications. Although it would seem to be a basic network function, batch-store-and-forward reduces the communication capacity required of an agency or company. Neither are required to support the telecommunications hardware to handle the peak communication periods. Communications are simplified. The agency or company does not have to dial and redial the other's computer because of a busy signal. The sender of the communication simply connects with IVANS and transmits its messages. The messages are held in the recipient's in basket until the receiver connects with IVANS to collect it.

The format conversion facility is another key feature offered by IVANS. This feature provides carriers with the ability to translate the data contained in the IIR transactions received from an agent into the form and sequence their computers expect it to be in. Where a carrier does not have an automated system, commercial lines for example, the format conversion facility can create a paper application which can be processed by the underwriter just as if it had been received through the mail. Carriers will also use the format conversion facility to translate the data they send to their interfaced agents into a form expected by the agents' computers, since not all agency systems will support every standard in the same way or at the same time.

The interactive communication feature allows agents and companies to use IVANS in a pass through mode for communications as a substitute for dedicated leased lines normally used for company terminals. The network may perform some protocol and speed conversions in the process, but will essentially allow an agency to view a company's online system on the agency's computer terminal. A terminal prompting and editing feature on the network is planned for the future. Terminal prompting will be a combination of interactive and batch-store-and-forward functions. The link between the agency and IVANS will be interactive. After the network computer has gathered the data through ACORD-like screens, it will be stored in IIR standard format in the designated company's IVANS in basket.

Reasons for Slow Implementation

IVANS is not proceeding as quickly as many had anticipated. While IVANS promises a number of benefits, other networks are available with many of the same features. Perhaps the major reason is a reluctance of both companies and agencies to begin using it. All of original technical specifications of the network have been implemented, but interest among potential agency and company clients to sign up for the system has not been as great as the IVANS staff originally anticipated. Agents are reluctant to sign up for the network because they are not sure if their companies are going to use the system. Conversely, insurance companies are hesitant to proceed with implementation because they do not see many of their agents preparing to send information through the network.

Not all of the carriers supporting development of the IIR standards are supporting IVANS. Several companies have established their own telecommunications networks. These companies are relectant to write off their large investments or subsidize their competitors' electronic access to independent agents, since this would eliminate the advantage they gained by their early entry into the market. In addition, those carriers with their own internal networks believe the cost of using IVANS will be much higher than that of their own networks. As a result, the IIR/ACORD membership will continue to be much higher than that of IVANS, since the need for some common industry electronic communication standard remains undeniable.

At this writing, it is too early to draw any firm conclusions about the future of IVANS. Although IVANS is an absolute necessity for the survival of those companies without their own networks in the automated world of tomorrow, IVANS will not be the only network available to the insurance industry. Competition will come from AT&T and one or more of the insurer/vendor networks already in place. Rather than sit back and wait to see how things turn out, many companies are in the process of implementing interface through IVANS. They expect to gain valuable experience from their pioneering communication projects with selected agents.

COMPUTERS, THE INSURANCE INDUSTRY, AND THE FUTURE

The chapter has thus far looked at past and current uses of

computers in the insurance industry. The last portion of this chapter will concentrate on the insurance industry's use of computers in the future.

Potential for the Insurance Industry

The potential for computerization in the insurance industry is enormous and indeed challenging. There are several concepts or goals that seem to capture the attention of those who observe the insurance data processing scene.

Paperless Processing Many vendors marketing to the insurance industry stress achievements toward the goals of paperless processing. The amount of insurance resources—money and labor—that goes toward managing the paper of the company makes clear why this is a worthwhile goal.

Advocates of paperless processing point to the concept that a piece of paper is merely one medium for storing information. Information in the insurance company has always been stored on paper—policy terms, changes to contracts, applications, and other related items. This is because paper has been, historically speaking, the favored medium for maintaining permanent records. Since computers can now store information more economically than it can be stored on paper, why not plan on the day when almost all information will be stored in the computer?

Some companies are moving quickly in this direction. Software vendors have made great strides in reducing companies' reliance on paper documents, but we are still a long way from paperless processing. The trend from transaction-oriented systems to policy-oriented systems was the first step toward this goal. Many companies achieved some relief from the paper avalanche by adopting microfilm data storage. Photographing and then reducing the image is essentially what is involved in microfilm and in microfiche, a similar technique. Many companies have shied away from it on grounds that it detracts from efforts toward automation through computers.

Image processing, under development for some time, offers hope to those who seek a paperless insurance company. Image processing involves the translation of the image of a piece of paper into a series of digits which can be stored in a digital computer. It will probably be a few years before image processing is generally affordable. Storage requirements are immense and will eventually be met by laser disk technology, much like that now used in compact audio disk players. Currently, a laser disk twelve inches in diameter can hold up to two billion characters, or the equivalent of more than a million double-spaced typewritten pages. Those who anticipate that image processing will be generally available in the next few years count heavily on continuation of the long trend toward increased computer storage hardware capacity at lower cost.

User-Directed System   Perhaps no other single development has been as interesting as the emerging role of end users. Insurance systems are no longer designed and implemented by just a few people in the company. Projects today are much too large and complex for that. Instead, users and data processors alike are working together on project teams to bring major system efforts to fruition.

Future systems are most likely to be user-directed to a great extent. This will be brought about, first of all, by widespread use of user-oriented programming languages. As these languages become more and more like the English language, a greater number of users will take advantage of them. This will lead to greater independence from the data processing department of the company. Users, conscious of growing pains and problems in past computer development, seem eager to deepen their involvement. As the fourth generation languages increase in their power, the trend toward user direction will be intensified.

Another factor adding to greater computer direction by users is the emphasis on distributed data processing. While user-oriented languages give the user the power to operate the computer, distributed data processing puts the computer where the user can take advantage of that power.

This picture is paradoxical, however. As systems are becoming more oriented to the user, they will, at the same time, become more complex; as user languages become more powerful, more functions will be added to the operating software, making the operating software more complex. That portion of the computer that must be used to keep the systems software operating (as opposed to the applications programs) is referred to as *overhead.* This overhead also increases as distributed data processing is implemented.

Granted that some of this overhead may be transferred away from the main computer location, it does not change the fact that the overall computer system has become more difficult to manage. Thus, users will be directing more of the system than ever before, but they will be limited to those options by the operating system software. Ultimately, control, as opposed to immediate usage, of systems will probably reside with fewer people rather than more.

The Electronic Office[8]   When does a typewriter stop being a typewriter and become a computer? The answer to this question lies in the additional functions that may be performed by the typewriter such as information storage or text editing. As computers become smaller, typewriters have grown larger—at least in the number of functions they provide. With the introduction of the IBM Magnetic Tape/Selectric typewriter in 1964, the word processing industry was off to a flying start. Since then innovations have come along rapidly. Some "typewriters" available today are actually small special-purpose minicomputers complete with video display.

Rising labor costs for clerks, typists, and similar workers have led to an increased demand for office machines, and rapidly developing computer circuit technology has led to an enticing array of devices. The whole idea of an electronic office is similar to, and related to, the concepts of agency-company terminal networks and paperless processing. Widespread use of Optical Character Recognition (OCR) equipment would allow documents to be read immediately into the computer system, in either the agent's or the underwriter's office. Computer output will be printed directly on microfilm for convenient long-term storage. Facsimile transmission allows documents to be transferred over telephone lines. Faster transfer times and, therefore, lower long distance telephone costs should lead to realization of the electronic mail concept. Voice communications through computers are seen as a future reality, and there are machines currently operational which "read" human voice patterns.

The future of the office in American business tends to arouse the imagination. Some fear the loss of the "personal touch" while others fear that automation will not come fast enough. This experience with computers and related equipment to date, however, suggests that technology will probably develop faster than our ability to manage it. The capabilities of computers are likely to exceed the ability to manage and effectively use those capabilities. The office of the future, therefore, waits not on the delivery of the machinery, but rather on the arrival of managers capable of its purpose.

MIS for the Insurance Company

Early attempts toward management information system development in the insurance industry generally resemble MIS development as a whole. There was, as expected, disenchantment with the MIS concept for some time among insurance company managers. This is changing as information database systems are being operated successfully by many companies. The success of software vendors, with their policy-oriented package programs, has also shown skeptics that there may yet be hope for the MIS concept, at least in some modified form.

Although on-line, policy-oriented systems are designed around processing needs, rather than management information needs, they do offer a base of data that can be fed to a controlling management information system. This is the concept, discussed in the previous chapter, of using a federation approach to MIS construction rather than a monolithic approach. At the least, these systems offer the groundwork for a management information system.

For many companies, the purchased database system is the chosen approach to MIS. This represents a "bottom-up" approach to MIS development. After mastering routine data processing functions, the information services staff can move "upward" into the area of management information. Although attending to processing needs first, the system collects much information that is management information as part of the process. After the bulk of processing data has been collected, the information services staff can work toward obtaining management information that is not already part of the database.

Other companies have taken the approach of utilizing the growing expertise of software vendors in developing a management information system. The underlying idea here is that the vendors will continue to increase the functions and overall capabilities of their systems. Moreover, the information retained in the systems, as with the more general database systems, will continue to grow in quantity and scope. With the vendor responsible for improving and maintaining this processing system, the company programming staff is free to concentrate on those computer information needs that are unique to the organization. In most cases, the unique needs will be management information needs.

As was stressed previously, the currently accepted way to MIS involves a federation of systems rather than a monolithic design. Regardless of the method used by the company (purchased database system, purchased applications software system, or company-developed systems), the federation approach seems to be the practice among insurers today. As these attempts meet with more success, interest in MIS within the insurance industry should intensify again.

Roadblocks to Progress

The pathway to increasing computerization in the insurance industry has both the initial allure and the ultimate perils of the yellow brick road. Before one can get to the Land of Oz, many hurdles must be overcome. Moreover, in the end, the wizardry promised by the computer may be found to have been an illusion fed by our insistent wish for it to be real.

If the term "roadblocks to progress" carries a negative connotation, consider the purpose for which roadblocks are designed. Highway roadblocks are not designed to cause inconvenience or discomfort for the motorist. They are designed to minimize inconvenience, for they warn of some peril in the road ahead. Sometimes, because of the peril, it is necessary to go a little out of the way before resuming course. At other times, it may even become necessary to change destinations. And so it is in the use of computers in the insurance industry. There are some roadblocks which must be analyzed to determine if they warrant major or minor shifts in the journey toward computerization. A few of them will be introduced here. The key work in the previous sentence is "introduced." The intent is to make the reader aware of the issues. Solutions will require much discussion and debate.

Lack of Industry Consensus   Public opinion notwithstanding, members of the insurance industry seldom agree on any subject. The industry is made up of numerous elements, each with its own identified interests. What is good for agents is not necessarily good for companies. What is good for stock companies is not necessarily good for mutual companies. What is good for direct writers is not necessarily good for commercial lines companies. And so it goes. This lack of consensus causes particular problems in the area of computerization. As mentioned earlier, the agency-company network poses many questions to those who urge its establishment.

Those who favor one network usually so do on the basis of the inefficiency of other approaches. There must be consensus in the industry if this common network is to be achieved. Many are now struggling to bring this consensus about. But not all agree that this consensus is either necessary or even desirable. Consider the problem from the viewpoint of the policyholder. With one network, cost could be kept lower because of the efficiency resulting from common network, procedures, codes, training requirements, and other factors. Presumably these cost savings would be passed on to the policyholder. Therefore, consensus in the development and operation of an insurance data communications network will benefit the insured. However, others argue that the consensus required to bring about standards in the insurance systems areas might bring about standards in areas where they are not desirable, decreasing competition.

If the insurance industry spoke with one voice, would the policyholder always benefit? Some say that the policyholder now benefits from the debate that goes on within the industry because insurance industry solutions are not imposed on the public by unanimous action. The competitive process might be hindered with a substantial increase in the number of industry standards. For example, assume that there were, suddenly, one computer system network that all companies could join. Would a small company have as much opportunity to compete and innovate as it now has? Not likely.

Security Concerns[9]   The subject of computer security has received much attention in the press. The concern for security of the computer and the information stored in the computer system is very much on the minds of corporate executives. As investments in computer hardware increase, concern should intensify.

Loss or damage to computers and their data can occur in several ways. Computers are subject to fire, lightning, and other familiar perils. Moreover, especially with the larger computers, sudden changes in temperature or humidity can result in loss. Vandalism is also a significant peril. Some destruction is done solely out of malice while some extremist groups, knowing the high potential for loss in data centers, destroy them to gain recognition. Many companies have installed expensive protective equipment to guard against these threats. No longer is the computer likely to be on display in a glass walled room. It may be placed in the most remote location possible. Computer crime also produces losses. Crimes, in some cases, are committed for the challenge of "beating the computer system" rather than for any monetary gain. Nevertheless, extremely large sums have been embezzled with the aid of computers.

The issue for the insurance industry, as well as other industries, is the trade-off between the savings of computerization and the chance of damage or loss of significant company information. Few people are willing to say that computerization should be halted to reduce the company's vulnerability to a major loss. Consider, however, some point to the enormous risk created when there is a centralized database with all corporate information. Despite elaborate security measures, there is still no absolute protection of the corporate database. What is an acceptable level of risk of theft, destruction, or misuse of the database? How can this risk be weighed against the competitive necessity and savings involved? Distributing the database (as under distributed data processing) reduces the problem but will not eliminate it. Because of our growing dependence on computers, future computer system designs will reflect a growing concern for computer and data security.

Privacy Concerns[10]   The issue of computer privacy has become a major public concern. It is commonly accepted that organizations require more information from us now than ever before. Government requirements for paper work from businesses have grown at a staggering rate. Insurance statistical organizations capture and maintain more information requirements. The development of the computer has made them possible. With the growing use of computer networks, many people are concerned about the misuse of information stored in computers which are now hidden from view.

Privacy legislation has been passed in the United States and in several western European countries. The concern for privacy is not new. What is new is the ability of government and sometimes other organizations to obtain and control large amounts of data about individuals through the use of computers. Personnel data stored in the computer might conceivably be assessed by an unauthorized party using a terminal.

Opinions on computer privacy tend to fall into one of three categories. First, there are those very concerned about the invasion of privacy possible with computers. Second, there are those who feel that the first group is making much ado about nothing and are more concerned about the cost and restraints that may be placed on computer departments due to privacy legislation. Third, many people are simply not aware of the magnitude of the issue.

Maintenance of privacy in computer systems costs money. Some argue that the privacy question should be decided on the basis of a cost/benefit analysis. The problem with this approach is putting a dollar figure on the benefits of maintaining the privacy of citizens. Insurance companies are and maintain a great deal of personal information about policyholders.

When discussing the agency-company terminal network idea, one must consider the rights of each policyholder to the privacy of personal information. Similarly, companies must not be able to extract private agency information from the network. And company pricing or financial data must not flow through to the network, to agencies, or to other insurers.

In a normal situation, privacy would probably not be difficult to safeguard, for each insurer will have a competitive interest in protecting its data. But what about an abnormal situation? It is difficult for many of us in this country to envision how an unscrupulous person or group might use large computer databases to influence or control portions of the population. While the idea seems farfetched, the possibility is a nagging specter. It is not the probability of personal data being misused that causes worry, but the mere possibility of major misuse of personal data stored in computers.

Those who develop insurance systems will have to consider this issue because of the legislation it has produced—if for no other reason. The insurance insurance will benefit, though, if thoughtful leaders step forward to provide guidance on this complex issue. The privacy issue provides the insurance industry with an opportunity to assert leadership in the business world in a matter of national importance.

Cost Allocation Agency-company networks will drastically change the process of providing insurance. The traditional allocation of functions between agent and company will be eroded as the computer enables—even compels—reassignment of some functions. For instance, the agent will perform more of the underwriting functions as the agency computer, interfaced with the insurer's computer, has access to information used in simple underwriting decisions. How much should the agent be "paid" for performing these functions? Obviously, agents will seek larger commissions when processing and storage functions are shifted from company to agency. Companies will seek to reduce commission rates as they perform decision, processing, and storage functions previously performed in the agency.

Cost allocation is a major issue in another way, too. The achievement of a full industry-wide agency-company interface will carry an enormous price tag. What is a fair split between companies and agencies? Should development costs be allocated to all firms in the insurance industry? Or should some firms be allowed a free (or, at least, cheap) ride as they follow in the footsteps of the brave?

TYPICAL DAY IN THE FUTURE

In tomorrow's automated agency, agency staff members will process their work through their own automated systems, moving in and out of multiple *windows* of information on their VDT screens. The windows will allow the agency staff to see and relate information from client, policy, loss, diary, note pad, word processing, and interface files on the VDT screen all at once. The windows will be moved around on the VDT screen, just as the agency staff now moves paper, and will be made larger, made smaller, or will disappear depending on the current task or inquiry from a client. As they are processed, those transactions which require action by a carrier will be identified for subsequent transmission to one or more companies and placed in the agency's interface out basket. At a convenient time during the day the accumulated transactions will be transmitted through local telephone lines to the closest IVANS access point for distribution to the companies to whom the transactions are addressed. From time to time, agency staff will activate various VDT windows on their workstations to obtain comparative rates based on information already contained in the system's client and policy files, to write letters and memos to insureds and prospects, or to project the results of today's events on the agency's financial position at some time in the future.

Periodically throughout the day, or at the end of each day, the companies will collect the accumulated transactions from IVANS and bring them in to their own internal automation systems. Prescreening or computer assisted underwriting systems will separate those transactions requiring manual review from the cons that can be processed without additional human intervention. The prescreening process will also generate requests for motor vehicle reports, credit and inspection reports, ISO survey data, and basic fire rates. Once the prescreening process is completed, the flow of transactions through the processing cycle of the company will be controlled by *queues*. The processing workload, identified by activity as it enters the company's automation system, will be queued for processing by underwriting, rating, claims or document processing. By searching the work queues, any underwriter will be able to determine his or her current workload. The underwriter can then schedule the work and proceed to process it.

The VDTs at underwriter workstations will also be divided into windows. The underwriter will move in and out of multiple windows to relate credit reports, inspection reports, agency comments and risk analysis, rating, diary, and scratch pad notes to the risk being evaluated. When presented with a complex commercial account, local underwriters will schedule telephone conferences to review the risk with more experienced underwriters through their respective VDT screens, no matter where they are located geographically. When underwriting has completed its evaluation of the transaction, the information will be placed in a rating queue. Rating will process its work according to effective change date. Using computerized rating systems, premium calculations and statistical codes will be developed after which the policy will be released for printing either within the company's location or directed for transmission to the agency for printing. Claim processing will be handled in a similar manner. Once the information request or transaction has been processed by the company, status information and any documents to be printed in the agent's office will be electronically communicated to IVANS or other networks for storage until collected by the agent's system. The agent's system will then update the client policy, and loss files as needed. The agency staff members will then be able to review the information through a window, their VDT screen, or print out the information, memos, policy documents, and forms on the agency's non-impact printer for distribution within the agency and mailing to the client.

As we see, the typical insurance office day in the future looks neither futuristic nor frightening. As Exhibit 3-4 illustrates, computers and networks, including those that provide interface between agencies and companies, will handle the messages. They will be the same messages that now flow along slower channels. This scenario shows a little room for the relocation of functions, but does not suggest any drastic shift of tasks from company to agency or vice versa. It promises major benefits: greater efficiency, economy, speed, and accuracy. One step at a time, the insurance industry will bring this scenario to life.

Exhibit 3-4
A Typical Day in the Future

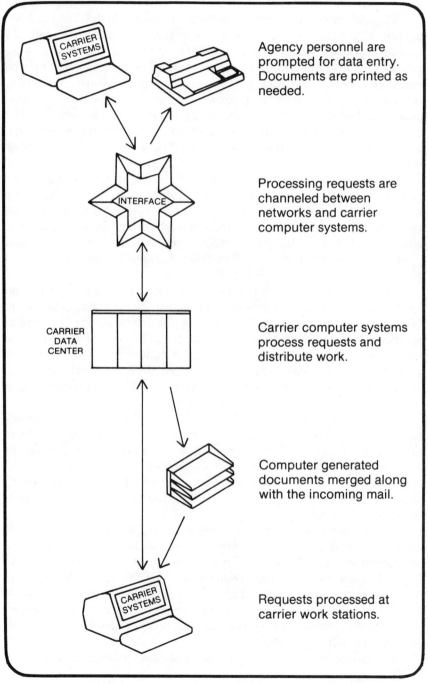

Agency personnel are prompted for data entry. Documents are printed as needed.

Processing requests are channeled between networks and carrier computer systems.

Carrier computer systems process requests and distribute work.

Computer generated documents merged along with the incoming mail.

Requests processed at carrier work stations.

SUMMARY

The history of the computer in the insurance industry has not been unique, but there are some ways in which the industry has made its special mark on the use of computers. Insurance companies were among the first to jump on the computer bandwagon. Having the necessary funds and the potential for major expense reduction, insurers stepped quickly to purchase the bulky and expensive computers of the late 1950s and the early 1960s. Many sensed that the computer could fill some very big needs within the insurance company, but few people realized that the computer field would develop as fast as it has.

Insurance companies are now among the major users of computer power. Sophistication has increased dramatically. From the early monofunctional systems to today's multi-purpose integrated systems the leaps have been nothing short of staggering. In the insurance company of today, the information services department (or data processing department, or information services department, or...) plays a role of enormous significance.

The insurance agent, aided by the growth of service bureaus and by the emergence of the minicomputer, joined the computerization race. With outside vendors providing most of the expertise for the typical smaller agent, computerization spread at a modest pace. With the development of cost-effective data communications networks, computer vendors have pursued the agency market almost with abandon. Perhaps the most discussed topic in insurance data processing circles today is the agency-company interface picture.

The potential for use of the computer in the insurance industry seems almost limitless because of the nature of the internal operations of insurers, large amounts of data flowing from one department to another. The computer offers the promise of reducing the problems associated with the high volume of paper work. Many look forward to paperless processing, realization of an effective MIS, the electronic office, and other concepts.

Yet without doubt some obstacles stand in the way of complete and effective computerization. The first of these is the inability to improve management and decision-making capacity at the same pace as improvements in computer technology. IVANS has delivered the nationwide agency/company data communications network the industry first asked for in 1978. The challenge for carriers and agency automation vendors is to develop the capability to use the network to improve the industry's efficiency.

The security, privacy, and cost allocation concerns which the computer causes must be dealt with while providing insurance policies and service in a competitive arena. It is almost certain that the insurance industry can survive as a private industry only if it can cut the costs of delivering its products. There seems to be no alternative to more effective computer utilization that will permit this reduction. All things considered, the insurance industry's future with the computer should be even more lively and interesting than its past.

Chapter Notes

1. Bernard L. Webb, J. J. Launie, Willis Park Rokes, and Norman A. Baglini, *Insurance Company Operations* (Malvern, PA; American Institute for Property and Liability Underwriters, 1978), Vol. I, p. 186.
2. Webb, Launie, Rokes, and Baglini, Vol. II, p. 278.
3. Webb, Launie, Rokes, and Baglini, Vol. I, p. 81.
4. Lawrence G. Brandon, *Sound a Clear Call* (Malvern, PA: CPCU-Harry J. Loman Foundation, 1984), p. 110.
5. James S. Burkart, "Computer Underwriting," *CPCU Annals*, March 1977, p. 69.
6. Independent Insurance Agents of America, National Association of Insurance Brokers, National Association of Insurance Women, Professional Insurance Agents, *Agency System Requirements: The Agent/Broker Viewpoint*, 1984.
7. Insurance Institute for Research, *Agency Automation Guide*, 1978.
8. Patricia Ancipin, "Some Perspectives on Electronic Office," *Best's Review* (Property/Casualty), May 1978, p. 78.
9. F. Warren McFarlan and Richard L. Nolan, eds., *The Information Systems Handbook* (Homewood, IL: Dow Jones-Irwin, Inc., 1975), pp. 832–842.
10. McFarlan and Nolan, pp. 843–856.

Glossary

Acoustic coupler—A device which allows a telephone to be used to provide communication from a terminal to a computer via a telephone network. An acoustic coupler is a type of modem that transfers information to a telephone line using sound impulses rather than direct electrical connection.

Add-on Memory—An additional primary storage unit attached to the CPU to, in effect, enlarge the size of primary storage.

ADP—See Automatic Data Processing

ALU—See Arithmetic/Logic Unit

Analog Computer—A computer that measures continuously variable data. Compare Digital Computer.

Applications Programming—Programming concerned with business problems as opposed to internal requirements of the computer. Compare Systems Programming.

Applications Software—Those programs that address business problems, such as accounts receivable, forecasting and word processing, as opposed to internal requirements of the computer. Compare Systems Software.

Arithmetic/Logic Unit—That unit within the CPU where arithmetic and logical comparison functions take place.

Artificial Intelligence—The ability of a computer to perform tasks characteristic of human intelligence, such as learning from experience and reasoning.

ASCII—American Standard Code for Information Exchange. The code used to represent letters, numbers, and other characters in data transmission.

Assembler—The software that translates a symbolic language program into a machine language program that the computer can process.

Assembler Language—A symbolic programming language. Each computer usually has its own assembler language.

Assembly Program—A computer program written in assembly language.

Asynchronous—A type of computer communication or a way of sending characters between parts of a system. Most widely used method for

157

connecting terminals to timesharing computers and connecting instruments to low-speed networks. Also generally used for connecting terminals and printers to small computers.

Automatic Data Processing—The field of computers and related work.

Auxiliary Memory—Storage media (for instance, disk or tape) other than primary storage.

Auxiliary Storage—Same as Auxiliary Memory.

Back-Up—(1) A copy of a computer file (tape, disk) that is retained in order to provide a means of recovery from system failure. (2) Back-up facility: another computer upon which programs can be run in the event of extended system hardware failure.

BASIC—(Beginner's All-purpose Symbolic Instruction Code) A procedure oriented programming language that is widely used in timesharing operations.

Batch—An accumulation of data that is considered a unit (as a day's sales) to be processed at one time in a computer system or communications network. Interactive processing is an alternative.

Batch Processing—Processing in which data is grouped and submitted to the computer in batches. Compare Real-Time processing.

Baud—For practical purposes, a term used in telecommunications as a unit of measure of data information flow. It stands for 1 *bit* per second. Divide by 8 to calculate characters per second.

Bisynchronous Transmission—A set of rules and procedures used by IBM (IBM Bisync) for controlling the message format. It specifies which data link control characters can be used for starting and ending a message.

Bit—Short for binary digit, that is, the smallest element of data in a computer.

Branch—The computer's ability to transfer from one part of a program (that is, to branch) to another part of the program based on the result of some comparison performed by the program.

Buffer—A part of a computer's memory where data can be stored until the computer is ready to process it. Some peripherals also have buffers.

Bugs—Any problems found in a software program which cause it to perform incorrectly.

Byte—A computer term for a character of information (D, 8, $, etc.). Computers are often compared in terms of memories expressed in thousands (K) or millions (megabytes—MB) of bytes. For example, a personal computer memory of 640K means that the computer's memory can hold approximately 640,000 characters.

Card Punch—A computer output device that produces the computer readable medium of punched cards.

Card Reader—A computer input device that reads punched cards.

Cassette Tape—A data medium on some computers.

Cathode-Ray Tube (CRT)—A television-like screen on which data can be displayed; a computer terminal with such a screen. Also called Video Display Terminal (VDT).

CBIS—See Computer-Based Information System.

Centralized Data Processing—Processing in which one host computer controls and services a network of mostly nonintelligent terminals.

Central Processing Unit (CPU)—The heart of a computer system consisting of primary storage, arithmetic/logic, and control units.

Channels—Computer devices supporting the operation of the computer system.

Chip—An integrated circuit or integration of many circuits on a wafer slice, most often silicon, which contains these circuits.

Closed-Shops—Computer rooms to which entry is restricted to a few employees for security reasons.

COBOL (COmmon Business Oriented Language)—The most common procedure-oriented language in use today.

Code—When a computer program is written it is often said to be coded. The written program instructions are called the code.

COM (Computer output to microfilm)—a technology combining electronic, photo-optical and electromechanical techniques for the purpose of converting digitized computer output into human-readable images and automatically recording these images on microfilm or microfiche.

Compiler—The software that translates a procedure-oriented language into machine language that the computer can execute.

Computer—A data processor that can perform computation, including numerous arithmetic or logic operations, without intervention by a human operator during the run.

Computer-Based Information System—An information system based primarily on data stored and managed by a computer.

Computer Science—The study of computers, with particular emphasis on their internal design and technological state.

Configuration—The design or layout of a particular computer system with all its peripherals. To configure a system is to design a system to meet specific needs. Can also mean to set certain hardware or software options in a manner which makes them compatible with the host.

Control Unit—That part of the central processing unit that exercises control over the functions performed by the computer.

Conversational—Same as Interactive.

Core—Another term for the primary storage of the central processing unit. The term reflects the fact that many storage units have had a magnetic core as the prime component.

CP/M—Acronym for Control Program for Microcomputers. A popular disk operating system used by many manufacturers. A trademark of Digital Research Corporation.

CPS—Acronym for characters per second. A measurement of speed of character transmission or printing.

CPU—See Central Processing Unit.

CRT—See Cathode-Ray Tube.

Cursor—A position indicator on a CRT, usually a flashing rectangle or underscore.

Daisy Wheel Printer—A printing device characterized by high quality, often referred to as a letter quality printer.

Data—Raw facts in isolation which, when placed in a meaningful context by a data processing operation(s), allow inference to be drawn. Compare Information.

Database—An organized collection of related files that contain data for the operation of an organization.

Data Center—That area or group of people responsible for physical maintenance, operations and security of the computer itself. Sometimes called Operations.

Data Communications—Operations which transfer data from one terminal or processor to another terminal or processor, usually through telephone lines or satellite technology.

Data Entry—The process of actually entering information into a computer system; for example, keying data into a terminal.

Data Processing—The field of computers and their related activity. Any procedure for receiving information and rearranging it to produce a specific result.

Data Processor—Any machine that performs operations with data.

DDP—Distributed Data Processing.

Debugging—The process of correcting a computer program, including detection of errors and subsequent resolution of problems.

Decision Tables—A documentation aid similar in purpose to a flowchart depicting in Matrix form (first) conditions that may occur in the program and (second) actions for the program to take based on the respective condition.

Dedicated Line—A telephone line used to transfer data in data communications that is leased and used solely for the purpose of transferring data between two points. A dedicated line eliminates the need for dialing and the connection is thus permanent until disconnected. Compare Dial-Up Line.

Development Programming—The phase when programs are being written for the first time. Compare Maintenance Programming.

Dial-Up-Line—A telephone line used to transfer data from one point to another. The connection is made by dialing the number of the computer or other processor to receive the data. Each time data is to be transferred, dialing (making a connection) is required. Compare Dedicated Line.

Digital Computer—Computer that performs computations on noncontinuous, discrete data (that is, it uses digits). Compare Analog Computer.

Direct Access—The ability to retrieve data elements without reading the entire data fire sequentially. Compare Sequential Access.

Direct-connect—Usually used with reference to modems, direct-connect describes a physical connection between the modem and modular telephone plug (as opposed to an acoustic connection, where a microphone and speaker connect to a telephone handset).

Disk—A metal or mylar disk with magnetic coating used to record information magnetically. Disk storage is the amount of information it can hold and is measured in millions (megabyte, MB) of characters.

Disk Drive—The device that contains and operates the disks.

Diskette (floppy disk)—A flexible mylar disk which is housed in a paper-like jacket. The data is stored magnetically but the total capacity is much less than that of a hard disk. Microcomputers generally use 5¼" diskettes which are single or double sided with single or double density storage capabilities.

Disk Operating System (DOS)—A program used by the computer to read, write and catalog disk files. Examples include MSDOS, CP/M, and TRSDOS.

Disk Pack—A removable, direct access storage device containing magnetic disks on which data are stored.

Distributed Data Processing—A network of computer(s) and terminals in which computer "intelligence" is placed in various terminals or computers throughout the network rather than being concentrated in one host computer. Compare Centralized Data Processing.

Documentation—The permanent record describing the logic and other pertinent facts relating to a program or system. It may consist of flowcharts, decision tables, or other written documents.

DOS—See Disk Operating System.

Dot Matrix Printer—(Wire Printer). A high speed printer that prints character-like configurations of dots through the selection of wire-ends rather than conventional characters through the selection of type faces.

Downtime—That time which is lost when computer equipment is not working because of some malfunction.

DP—See Data Processing.

Drum Storage—A storage medium similar to disk storage but less commonly used. Storage is achieved by selective magnetization of portions of the surface of a cylinder.

Dumb Terminal—A computer terminal with no processing capabilities of its own. Compare Intelligent Terminal.

Edit—A check performed by the computer or computer program for errors in data entered.

EDP—See Electronic Data Processing.

EFT—See Electronic Funds Transfer.

Electronic Cottage—See Telecommuting.

Electronic Data Processing—The field of electronic computers and their operation.

Electronic Funds Transfer—A banking concept allowing money to be transferred through a computer network utilizing data communications and eliminating much paper work.

Electronic Mail—Mail sent in electronic form, not on paper.

End User—Persons who use computer outputs in an organization excluding members of the data processing department.

Ergonomics—The study of anatomical, physiological and psychological aspects of people in their working environments.

Expert Systems—Computer programs that act as expert consultants to users. It consists of three components; a base of knowledge supplied by an expert in the field, a set of facts supplied by the user and a inference capability supplied by the program.

Facilities Management—Usually involves the subcontracting of an organization's entire data processing to another firm.

Floppy Disk—See Diskette.

FORTRAN (FORmula TRANslation)—A very popular scientific-mathematic programming language.

Fourth Generation Languages—Languages that do not require the user to specify how to do everything to obtain the desired information from a computer. Instead, a compiler makes assumptions about what the user needs.

Front-End Controller—Computer program used to off-load the central processing unit by performing basic polling of all terminals in the network, relieving the CPU for other work.

General Purpose Computer—A computer able to perform a variety of functions. Compare Special Purpose Computer.

Generations—Term used to describe stages in the development of computers and their technology. Most analysts agree that there have been four or five generations of computers since they were introduced in the 1950s.

GO TO—Computer instruction that enables branching. The computer, when certain conditions occur, is able to *Go To* or *Branch To* some other part of the program.

Hard Copy—A computer printout on paper.

Hardware—Physical computer equipment. Compare Software.

High-Level Languages—Same as Procedure-Oriented Languages.

Host Computer—The controlling computer in a network of computer(s) and terminals.

Hybrid Computer—Computer with the characteristics of analog and digital computers.

Hybrid Processing—Processing which combines features of batch and online processing.

Icon—Method of interfacing with a computer using icons (symbols) to represent procedures or devices desired.

Information—The increase in knowledge obtained by the recipient by matching the proper data elements to the variables of a problem. Information is the aggregation or processing of data to provide knowledge or intelligence. Compare Data.

Information Center—(in large organizations) a department that offers aid to organization members in using their own information processing resources.

Information Processing—The field of computers and their management, particularly as it relates to business information systems.

Ink-jet Printer—Non-impact printer that produces dot-matrix characters by spraying droplets of ink to form images.

I/O—Input/Output—Internal links in a computer used to get information to and from parts of the system itself.

Input—Data being entered into a system by a data entry device such as a CRT or by copying from a magnetic storage device such as a disk or tape.

Intelligent Terminals—Computer terminals which have the capability to perform some limited processing functions normally reserved for the computer itself. Compare Dumb Terminals.

Interactive Processing—Processing performed from a terminal with frequent person-machine interaction. As the computer receives input, it presents questions or instructions to the user, such as instructions for the next item of data to be entered.

Interface (general sense)—The electronic exchange of information.

Interface (in the insurance industry)—Electronic exchange of information between an agency computer system (true interface) or terminal and the computer of an insurance company.

Internally Stored Program—A sequence of computational steps. It is the ability to hold an internally stored program that distinguishes a computer from any other information handling machine (for example, an adding machine).

Job—A series of data processing steps or operations performed in succession as a unit of work to complete a given task.

"K"—A metric term for 1,000 (kilo). In computer applications, however, it means 1,024 bytes or characters. Used most often when stating memory capacity. ("128K" means 131,072 bytes of memory.)

Keypunch—A keyboard device that punches holes in a card to represent data.

LAN (Local Area Network)—A system for linking various computer devices together over a relatively small geographic area.

Lead Operator—The computer operator in charge of a shift, also called Shift Supervisor.

Leased Line—Same as Dedicated Line.

Line Printer—A high speed printer that prints a line at a time versus a character at a time like a dot matrix or letter quality printer. Its speed is referred to in Lines Per Minute (300 LPM).

Local—When applied to computer hardware, refers to those devices that are in the immediate vicinity of the central processing unit. Compare Remote.

Machine Language—The language that the computer actually "understands."

All other languages must be reduced to this level before the computer can execute instructions.

Magnetic Core—An individual magnetic core is a tiny doughnut-shaped ring of ferrite capable of being magnetized in one or two states at any given moment. Thousands of these tiny rings were strung together to form primary storage in many third generation computers.

Mainframe—(1) Same as Central Processing Unit. (2) An organization's main computer system.

Main Memory—Same as Primary Storage.

Maintenance Programming—Changing, that is, correcting or improving, existing programs. Compare Development Programming.

Management Information System—A group of people, a set of manuals, and data processing equipment that select, store, process, and retrieve data to reduce the uncertainty in decision making by yielding information for managers at the time they can most efficiently use it.

Matrix Printer—See Dot Matrix Printer.

Megabyte—One million bytes (characters). Usually used when speaking of disk storage.

Media—The means for storing computer readable data, including magnetic tape, disk, and cards.

Microcomputer—Smallest type of data processing system available today; called personal computer (PC).

Microprocessor—A chip that contains complete processing circuitry.

Microprogramming—The technique of controlling various functions of the computer with pseudo-instructions already integrated into the computer circuits.

Minicomputer—A computer which is larger than a microcomputer. It is more expensive, may need special air conditioning or power, but has more storage capability.

Mnemonic Symbol—A symbol chosen to assist the human memory. For example, the symbol "prem" may represent "premium."

MODEM—A MODulation/DEModultation device that connects a computer to a telephone line in order to exchange information.

Mouse—A hand held pointing device used to control the cursor on a VDT.

Network—The communication vehicle for a computer equipped with the proper communication hardware to interface (send/receive) data with other interconnected computers at multiple locations.

Nonprocedural Languages—A language that tells a computer what is to be accomplished. The compiler then determines how to do what has been asked. Compare Procedural Languages.

Object Program—Program in machine language. The programmer prepares a source program in an easy-to-use symbolic or procedure-oriented language and then assembles or compiles it into the object program.

Off-line—Computer operations performed without direct operator intervention. For example, printing invoices at night.

Off-Loading CPU—Removing functions normally performed by the central processing unit and putting them in some supporting device such as a front-end controller.

Online Processing—This requires that computer terminals be attached to the computer, usually through telephone lines, and that they be able to access information in the computer as well as input information to the computer at any time desired by the terminal user. Normally, when any device is connected directly with the computer it is said to be online.

Op Code—See Operation Code.

Operating System—The group of programs that together controls the physical operations of the computer and the movement of data between the parts of the system. This is the major component of systems software. A compiler is part of the operating system.

Operation Code—That portion of the computer instruction that denotes the operation to be performed (for example, addition, subtraction). Normally applies only in machine and symbolic languages.

Operations—The group of people or department charged with the responsibility of physical maintenance, operation, and security of the computer itself.

Operator's Console—An input/output device which is used by the computer operator when specific instructions are needed to operate the computer itself.

Optical Character Reader—A computer input device that recognizes symbols printed on objects (for example, food cans at the grocery store) according to a standard coding scheme.

Output—Data disseminated by a computer to a device such as a CRT, printer, or disk.

Password—A code known only to the computer system and authorized users that permits the computer to refuse access to any user who does not reply with the proper code word.

Peripherals—All computer hardware devices other than the central processing unit.

Plug-Compatible—Computer equipment produced to operate compatibly with IBM equipment. There are plug-compatible tape drives, disk drives, etc.

Polling—The process by which the central processing unit checks each terminal on the computer network sequentially to see if activity is desired by that terminal. This process must go on constantly while terminals are online and, of course, must proceed at a very high rate of speed.

Ports—Sockets used by computers to pass data to and from other devices. There are different types of ports. Serial ports pass information one "bit" at a time. Parallel ports pass multiple bits of information, usually one "byte" at a time.

Primary Storage—That part of the central processing unit designed for storage of programs and data which are being used by the computer at a given moment. New programs and data are constantly brought into primary storage as other programs and data are no longer needed.

Procedure-Oriented Language—A computer language that requires the programmer to specify exactly how the computer is to perform something. (For example, COBOL or BASIC).

Processor—Same as Central Processing Unit.

Program—A sequence of computational steps to be performed on data in order to perform a specific function.

Program Libraries—Collections of various programs. They are stored in the computer for use when the operator calls for them.

Program Listing—Same as Compilation Listing.

Programmer—A person who designs, writes, and tests computer programs.

Programmer Analyst—A data processing job which combines the functions of a programmer with those of a system analyst.

Project Management—A method (used in some programming departments) which assigns programmers to a project for the duration of that project.

Prompt—A programming technique applied to data entry whereby the operator is assigned or guided in his task by the appearance of messages or indicators displayed on his data entry device.

Protocols—A description of the method used to transmit and receive information between communicating devices.

Query Languages—Computer languages which allow users to become more involved in the programming function than procedure-oriented languages do.

RAM—Random Access Memory. Memory in the computer that holds application programs while they are being run. It is erasable so when a progam is finished, another program can be run using the same memory.

Random Access—Same as Direct Access.

Real-Time Processing—A specific type of online processing wherein the user has direct access to the computer and its files, and can use those files directly and immediately within the time required for an external event (for example, real-time processing provides immediate computer confirmation of a reservation).

Remote—Those devices—usually terminals—that are removed from the immediate vicinity of the central processing unit. Compare Local.

Remote Job Entry—The process of entering programs for compilation and subsequent execution at a remote terminal (a card reader and printer are the usual equipment involved).

Remote Processing—A type of service provided by vendors wherein terminals are installed at the user location and are connected by telephone lines to the vendor's computer.

Report Writers—Languages designed so that an end user can define certain parameters from which the report writer will then generate a program that will produce the desired report.

Response Time—In an interactive mode of operation, the lapsed time between the end of the input and the beginning of the output.

RJE—See Remote Job Entry.

ROM—Read Only Memory. Non-erasable memory used to store instructions that are always needed by the computer such as built-in diagnostics.

RPG—(Report Program Generator)—a report writer language that is very popular in business.

Run—A sequence of computational steps to be performed on the data. Often used synonymously with program.

Security—Methods used to prevent unauthorized access to part or all of the information in a data base.

Semiconductor Memory—A type of computer memory utilizing silicon chips for its computer circuits.

Sequential Access—An access method whereby individual data elements cannot be retrieved without reading the entire file in sequential order. Data stored on magnetic tape must be retrieved by sequential access. Compare Direct Access.

Service Bureau—A data processing vendor that normally provides contract systems analysis, programming, some data entry functions, and produces production runs.

Software—The programs needed to operate the computer system as distinguished from the physical machines. Compare Hardware.

Software House—A vendor that produces and markets software packages and provides contract programming services.

Source Code—Those statements a programmer writes in a particular language (COBOL, BASIC, etc.) to create an application program.

Special Purpose Computer—A computer designed for a special or limited purpose. Compare General Purpose Computer.

Spooler—A software package that uses buffer storage to control input/output and processing activities. Spooling allows one job to run while another is being printed.

Stand Alone Mode—A computer operating without the control or support of some other computer.

Stored Program Concept—The idea that a computer can retain an internally stored program. Once the sequence of steps has begun, no subsequent intervention is required.

Structured Programming—Writing programs according to a set of rigid rules in order to decrease testing problems, increase productivity, and increase the readability of the resulting program.

Symbolic Language—High level language developed as a solution to some of the problems associated with programming in machine language; utilizes mnemonic codes and macro instructions.

Synchronous—A type of computer communication in which messages are sent from one device to another within a specified length of time. Both devices must be "synchronized" in order to communicate. Most often used when large volumes of data must be transferred.

System—A computer and its associated peripheral devices (hardware) and programs (software). Also used for the combination of hardware and software designed to perform specific or multiple functions, such as an agency management system.

System Analyst—The person who specifies the scope and characteristics of programs and series of programs.

Systems Programming—Programming concerned with the internal operations of the computer as opposed to business problems. Compare Applications Programming.

Systems Software—Those programs that manage the internal operation of the computer rather than solve business problems. Compare Applications Software.

Tape Drive—The physical device that reads from and writes on magnetic tape.

Telecommunications—Data transfer over telephone or teletype lines from one terminal or processor to another. Basically the same as Data Communications.

Telecommuting—A work arrangement in which employees stay home all or most of the time and use computer terminals or microcomputers to process data and then communicate the results to the office.

Teleprocessing—Data processing by means of a combination of computers and data communications facilities to process information to and from remote locations.

Teleprocessing Monitor—Software that operates under the control of the operating system and acts as a "mini-operating system" for those programs that are servicing interactive terminals in a computer network.

Terminal—A device attached to a computer that allows either input of data, output of data, or both. Usually consists of a VDT and keyboard.

Timesharing—A form of computer processing involving the simultaneous use of a number of computer terminals. Although many terminals may be served simultaneously, it appears to the terminal user that he or she is the only user of the computer.

Turnkey System—A system is said to be a "turnkey" if a single vendor provides the purchaser with hardware, software, and maintenance as a package.

Update—Processing transactions against a file so that it will reflect the latest status of the information.

Upgrading—Replacing a computer or computer system with more powerful or more sophisticated hardware and/or software.

User Friendly—A description applying to a system that is particularly easy for an operator to use. Characteristically, it provides for operator prompting and the use of mnemonics and reduces the need for reference to external documentation such as manuals or operator guides.

User-Oriented Language—Languages that allow for more user involvement and control than that allowed by Procedure-Oriented Languages. Usually restricted in use to producing simple files and reports although their sophistication is increasing. Compare Fourth-Generation Languages.

Users—Usually refers to those people a computer serves; the data users rather than the computer operators. Same as end user.

Value Added Network—A network which, in addition to moving data from point to point, enhances the quality of the data being transmitted.

VDT—Video display terminal; same as CRT.

Verifying—In batch processing, the step of checking the validity of data already encoded onto punched cards or some other medium.

Virtual Memory—An operating system technique that allows auxiliary storage to be treated as if it were primary storage, effectively increasing the capacity of the central processing unit without the addition of physical storage in the CPU.

Window—One or more subdivisions of a VDT screen that can be expanded and contracted as needed by the user; a window allows diplay of information different from that on the rest of the screen.

Index

C

T

U

V

W